The Band Director's Guide to
INSTRUMENT REPAIR

The Band Director's Guide
to
INSTRUMENT
REPAIR

R.F. "Peg" Meyer

Edited By Willard I. Musser

ALFRED PUBLISHING CO., INC.
PORT WASHINGTON, NEW YORK

ISBN: 0-88284-002-9
Library of Congress Catalog Card Number 72-96638
Printed in the United States of America

Alfred Publishing Co., Inc.
75 Channel Drive, Port Washington, New York 11050

INTRODUCTION

Consider this astonishing fact: a great number of school band directors get only 75 per cent—or less—performance efficiency from students' musical instruments and do absolutely nothing about it.

This is obviously unacceptable—at any time. But such deficiency is even more glaring in the light of today's technology. For the average listener, more conscious of tone quality through experience with fine music-producing units, is far less content with mediocrity. Accordingly, school bands are expected to provide quality performances, an ideal that can be achieved and maintained *only* when instruments are in perfect playing condition.

This book is therefore designed as a convenient and, most important, *practical* repair guide for teachers and band directors; a step-by-step presentation to help you find and correct an extensive range of musical-instrument malfunctions.

Like many other mechanical devices, a musical instrument is subject to wear and deterioration during its entire service life, starting with the first use. Directors frequently censure students for failing to develop embouchure and breath control, attributing poor performance to insufficient practice. However, the instrument itself may well be at fault. For tone quality and overall performance can be seriously affected by any of a number of conditions or malfunctions.

For example:

■ If clarinet or saxophone mouthpieces are not cleaned regularly, foreign matter collects on the interior surfaces, which retain moisture. When the individual mouthpiece is covered with its cap (reed intact) and then placed in the case—which is practically airtight—the reed deteriorates in strength and, consequently, in tone-producing capabilities.

■ When clarinet toneholes become lined with oily dirt from fingers, this condition not only affects tone quality, but also pitch. Baggy pads extending into the toneholes produce the same adverse effects, while uneven tonehole rings not only cause inaccurate tones, but also make positive trilling almost impossible.

■ The height of the action (distance between pads and tone-holes) on saxophones will affect the pitch, and if the entire line of action is not even the instrument will be out of tune with itself.

■ The tone quality of a cornet section can be greatly affected by bent mouthpiece shanks and dirty leadpipes. As much as a teaspoon of food particles, lime, dirt, and foreign matter can frequently be removed by running a swab through one mouthpipe. If the valve ports are lined with dirt or corrosion, if the water key corks leak, or if the felts and corks on the valve stems are deteriorated so the ports do not align correctly, the tone quality will be affected.

■ Trombone players clean the inside of the outer slide so the slide will work properly; few, however, clean the inside of the inner slide, which collects all the foreign matter blown in with the saliva. Remove the outer slide and hold the inner slide up to the light; then glance through it. You'll be amazed at what you see!

This description of just a few of the conditions that impair tone and performance is also intended to impress you with the fact that a periodic check of each instrument is critical. A time-consuming procedure, of course, but one that is absolutely essential. Total band sound, even when comprised of many good tones, can be labeled as faulty as a result of only one defective tone.

Therefore, a thorough inspection of each instrument at least once a month is strongly recommended. When malfunctions are uncovered and all instruments restored to their original playing capabilities, you will find an enormous improvement in overall band performance.

INSTRUMENT QUICK-CHECK ROUTINE

Just before a performance, a band director may be approached —as many are—by a student who frantically exclaims that his instrument does not work. At such time, a director urgently needs the quickest possible method of locating the difficulty. Accordingly, a quick-check routine, with check points listed in order of importance and occurrence, will be found at the end of the detailed repair section for each instrument. The routines provide a conservative checking system for general instrument repairs.

Note: The word *pedal* will be used throughout this book to describe any key action or key part which is pressed by the finger to initiate an action.

The part of a key pressed by the finger to operate a French horn valve is sometimes called the "spatula"; however, this term could also be used to classify various keys on the clarinet, saxophone, and flute. The side trill keys on a clarinet would not be classified as spatulas because of their size and shape; therefore, a more relevant term is used: pedal.

CONTENTS

The Band Director's Guide to
INSTRUMENT REPAIR

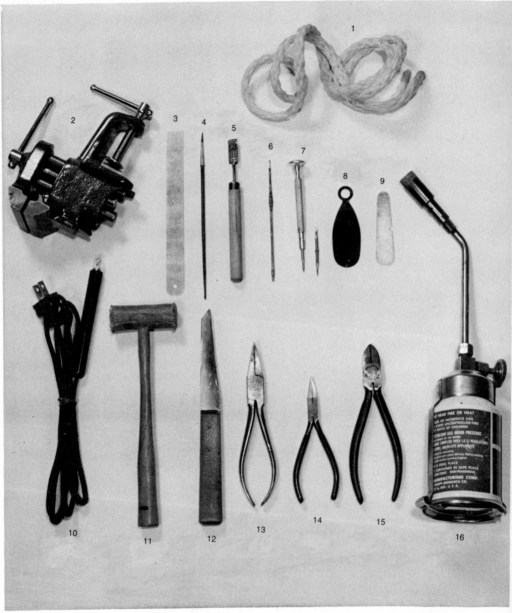

Photo 1.
Among the supplies and tools listed in Chapter 1 are those illustrated here:

1. Braided synthetic pull rope
2. Bench vise
3. Ruler with 32nds and millimeters
4. Small watercolor brush
5. Shellac iron
6. Spring hook
7. Screwdriver
8. Flute pad iron
9. Pad slick
10. Leaklight
11. Rawhide mallet
12. Bench knife
13. Large flatnose pliers
14. Small flatnose pliers
15. Cutting pliers
16. Propane torch

1

SUPPLIES, TOOLS, AND BASIC PARTS

The following supplies and tools are essential for the procedures described in this Repair Guide.

SUPPLIES

Tube of cement (shellac) or flake shellac and alcohol (Contact cement might be preferred for certain specific jobs)
Water key corks
Valve corks, felts, and bumpers
Water key springs
Sheets of $^1/_{64}''$, $^1/_{16}''$, $^3/_{32}''$ and $^1/_8''$ cork
Penetrating oil
Key oil
Silencer skins
Springs (See each instrument section for spring types)
Sheet of fine-grain sandpaper or #220 emery cloth
Pumice
Pads (See each instrument section for pad types)
Small roll of 1-inch adhesive tape
Stick of French horn cork (for stop arms)
Rubber bands, size #33
French horn valve string
Stick of shellac

TOOLS

Rawhide mallet
Pad slick
Two screwdrivers or one with interchangeable bits
Long-neck screwdriver for saxophone repairs
Flatnose pliers (small and large)
Longnose pliers
Spring hook (can be made with #7 or #8 crocheting needle)
Small bench vise (plain jaws)
Small watercolor brush or hypodermic needle-type oiler
Leaklight
Sax testing light (also fine for Flutes and Bass Clarinets)
Propane torch, and Bunsen burner or alcohol lamp
Flute pad iron
Shellac iron
Bench knife (cork knife)
Cutting pliers (for shortening springs, etc.)
Ruler with 32nd inch and millimeter markings
Braided synthetic pull rope
Small file (magneto type)

AUXILIARY TOOLS

Hook scraper (for removing cork from tenons, cleaning metal
   for soldering, and removing excess solder after soldering)
Spring pliers (with open slot on one jaw for removing and
   inserting needle springs)
Roundnose pliers (for straightening key cups and sax and
   flute toneholes)
Jeweler's anvil (for flattening springs, straightening pad cups,
   and setting pads)
Hard-faced bench or mechanic's hammer (for flattening
   springs)

SCREWBLOCK

When the removal of clarinet keys is necessary, a screwblock
will conveniently systematize the arrangement of pivot and hinge
screws.

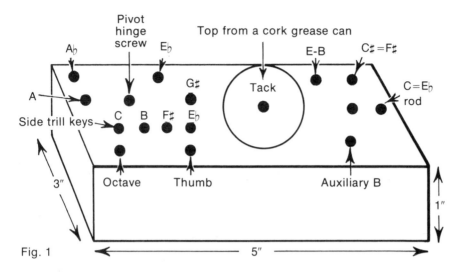

Fig. 1

Construction directions: Start with a wood slab 1 inch thick, 5 inches long, and 3 inches wide. Following the pattern in the figure shown here, drill holes about ³/₄ inch deep with a ¹/₃₂-inch bit. Notice that the screw arrangement is similar to that of the clarinet. Anchor the lid from a cork grease container to the center of the block with a tack; use this to contain the pivot screws.

Even if you are removing only a few screws, be sure to use the screwblock and place the screws in their proper places. This will eliminate considerable hunting and confusion.

SPRING HOOK

A serviceable spring hook can be fashioned easily from a #7 or #8 crocheting needle.

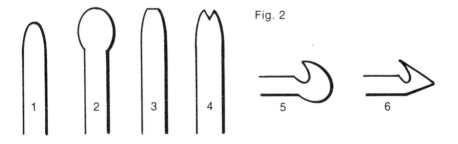

Fig. 2

Construction directions: Take the rounded end of the needle (1) and flatten it with a hammer (2). File this end down so that the tip is flat and the body is slightly tapered at the end (3). Now file or cut a groove in this tip (4). Next, take the hook end of the needle (5) and file off bulges (6).

RAWHIDE MALLET

Photo 2

A rawhide mallet will prove to be one of your most useful tools. Some repairmen prefer to "roughen up" the mallet faces until they are soft enough to prevent marring. Note the faces in photo 2—they're fuzzy. This effect can be created by striking the mallet repeatedly against a sharp edge (e.g., a bench vise). After the mallet faces acquire this condition, they will not scratch or mar the finish of brass instruments when the mallet is used to loosen lodged slides, mouthpieces, valve caps, etc.

KNIFE BOARD

A good way to keep your bench knife sharp is by using a knife board, which consists of fine emery cloth on one side, leather on the other.

Fig. 3

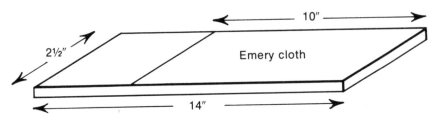

Construction directions: Start with a piece of wood about $1/4$ inch thick, 2-$1/2$ inches wide and 14 inches long. Cover (secure with glue) 10 inches of one side with fine-grain emery cloth and 10 inches of the other side with Crocus cloth. First strop the knife on the emery side and finish on the Crocus side. Use the uncovered section as a handle.

BASIC INSTRUMENT PARTS

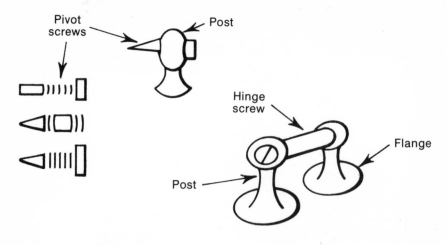

Pivot screws

Post

Hinge screw

Post

Flange

Pivot hinge screw

Bridge keys

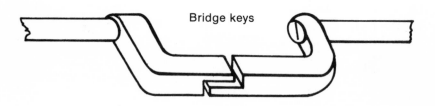

Ligature or neck screw

Flute rod wedge pin

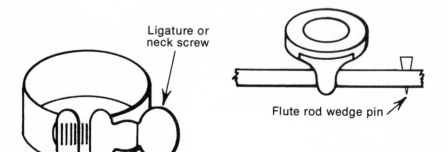

Threads   No threads

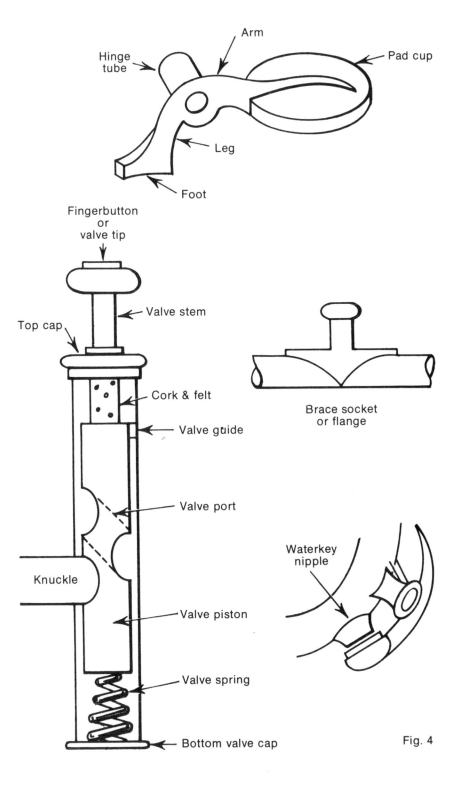

Arm

Hinge tube

Pad cup

Leg

Foot

Fingerbutton or valve tip

Valve stem

Top cap

Cork & felt

Valve guide

Brace socket or flange

Valve port

Waterkey nipple

Knuckle

Valve piston

Valve spring

Bottom valve cap

Fig. 4

CHAPTER

PRECAUTIONS

Some emphatic precautions: study carefully and review thoroughly before attempting to repair any instrument.

GENERAL

Do not attempt to repair a musical instrument until you have isolated the malfunction. The most successful doctor is the best diagnostician; the same is true in your role as a musical instrument repairman.

Do not do anything to a musical instrument in front of your students that you wouldn't want them to do or know about.

Do not use an abrasive cleaner or glass wax to clean the inside of gold-plated bells. The gold plating is very thin and can be removed easily.

Do not allow students to make repairs (remove lodged slides, bend keys, etc.) unless they have been instructed in the proper procedure.

Do not allow students to chew gum or eat candy while playing an instrument. Sugar impairs valve action and causes pads to stick —especially flute and saxophone G♯ key pads, which have light spring action.

Do not take it for granted that students will clean and service their musical instruments on their own initiative. Encourage good maintenance habits.

WOODWIND INSTRUMENTS

Do not attempt to assemble a wood instrument when its rings are loose.

Do not bend a key to compensate for play between the parts due to a missing piece of cork or felt. Many woodwind instrument keys are activated by the unison movement of a combination of keys. These keys have a piece of cork or felt at their point of contact to eliminate any metallic click or vibration. Bending a key will only prevent the next key from working and, eventually, the entire action will be out of adjustment. (The body of this book lists all trouble spots, what to look for, and how to correct specific problems.)

Do not boil plastic or hard rubber mouthpieces to sterilize them. Hot water will warp the facings.

Do not use rubber bands on silver-plated instruments to hold keys closed or to hold keys with broken springs open. Rubber contains sulfur which will eat through the plating in a few weeks.

Do not fail to tell your woodwind players to wash their mouthpieces with soap and water at least once a week.

Do not put oil or grease on pads to waterproof them. Oil evaporates slowly and will saturate the pads, causing them to shrink and fall out.

Do not fail to oil all rods, screws, and springs immediately after cleaning an instrument with polish. Most polishes contain an ingredient that, although not harmful to brass, silver, or German silver, will rust steel (the material used for rods, screws, and springs).

Do not put powder on pads to prevent them from sticking. For best results, remove the material that is causing the trouble. Place a clean piece of cloth between the pad and tonehole; press the key very lightly; then draw the cloth out from under the depressed pad, thus cleaning the pad and tonehole surface at the same time.

Do not use ordinary glue, mucilage, or any other adhesive soluble by water to install pads, bumpers, corks, or felts. Humid weather, saliva, condensation of breath, or perspiring hands will soften the adhesive and expel the pad.

Do not heat a pad cup with a lighter or match to secure a pad if you know that the pad has previously been "floated in." If the cup contains French cement and a thin pad is used, excessive heat will force the cement out from under the pad. Never try to secure a pad in a piccolo in this manner, since most piccolo pads are "floated in" and disturbing the cement will prevent the pad from seating.

BRASS INSTRUMENTS

Do not use pliers to remove a lodged mouthpiece from a brass instrument. You will not only mar the mouthpiece but may break the braces and twist the mouthpipe. Remember that brass is soft and bends easily.

Do not use a door jamb or vise to twist a lodged mouthpiece. The seal of the lodged mouthpiece is stronger than the mouthpipe tubing or braces, which bend very easily. (Many cornets and trumpets frequently require new mouthpipes because someone thought the latter procedure "might" work.)

Do not attempt to dislodge a main trumpet slide by placing the inside of the bell on your kneecap and then pulling on the slide. This may collapse the bell at about the first brace.

Do not attempt to dislodge slides while the valves are out of the casings. This may spring the casings.

Do not try to dislodge a valve by forcing an ice pick or any other pointed object through the hole in the bottom valve cap—you will puncture the valve-port lining.

Do not use pliers or a pipe wrench to remove binding valve caps, since brass is soft and will mar easily. Tap the caps with a rawhide mallet until you break the seal; then they will unscrew easily.

Do not stretch valve springs to make the valves work more efficiently; clean the valves and casings.

Do not try to do a super-cleaning job by soaking your lacquered instrument in a cleaning solution. The chemical reaction that occurs is most likely to discolor the entire instrument.

Do not allow a student to play a new trombone before the slides are lubricated.

Do not fail to loop the rag back over the eyelet of a rigid trombone cleaning rod. Metal against metal can easily produce ridges in the slide.

Do not use a short rag on your rigid trombone cleaning rod; use one long enough so that it does not entirely enter the slide. This will provide a tab for pulling the rod out, in the event that it becomes lodged when turned.

Do not try to burn out a lodged rag by holding the slide over a flame. Twist the rod and gradually push forward as you twist. This will wrap the rag tighter on the rod, making it smaller. Keep twisting as you withdraw the rod. If the rag comes off the rod, blow it out with an air hose.

Do not allow a student to play a new valve instrument before the valves have been lubricated.

Do not allow students to drink anything containing an acid—such as lemon or lime—and then play an instrument without a lubricant on the valves and slides. In the event this happens and valve trouble occurs, wash the valves and casings with water, which will dissolve any sugar. Then apply the oil. Oil alone will not dissolve sugar.

Do not attempt to straighten a bent bell. If a bent trombone or trumpet bell has a crease at the bend, as shown here,

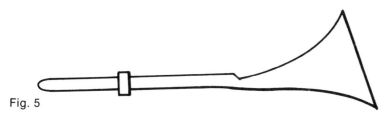

Fig. 5

do not try to straighten the bell by forcing it in the opposite direction. If it is forced, the opposite side of the tubing will collapse.

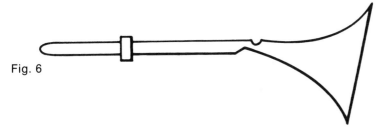

Fig. 6

A deep crease will usually crack the metal, which means replacing the bell. A professional repairman is better equipped to handle such problems. By using a mandrel, he will probably be able to straighten the bell so the bend is not even noticeable. Students should *not* attempt to straighten a bell if it is bent accidentally. Under pressure, an individual's strength can become overwhelming, but such power is not an asset in this instance.

CHAPTER

SPRINGS

Springs are an important part of a musical instrument. They hold keys open, hold keys closed, push valves up, turn valves around, and respond to the instrumentalist's commands concerning rate of speed and extent of force desired.

Springs are made of bronze, steel, iron, and even gold, and appear in a variety of shapes. All springs have one thing in common: they exert either a pushing or pulling force.

WOODWIND INSTRUMENT SPRINGS

Woodwind instruments use needle and flat springs. Flat springs, which are secured to the key by a flat spring screw, are used in two ways: (1) mounted in front of the hinge to pull keys closed, or (2) mounted behind the hinge to push keys closed. Notice where the spring is attached so you will know where to strengthen it if the key action becomes weak.

Strengthening Springs: (1) Spring mounted in front of the hinge: bend the spring tip down. (2) Spring mounted behind the hinge: the bend will be nearer to where the spring is attached to the key.

Replacing Needle Springs: Needle springs have a pointed end and a flattened end, and are installed by wedging the flat end into the hole in the post. Springs are obtainable in many lengths and diameters. Although it is not necessary, of course, to stock all sizes and types, it is recommended that you have on hand one set of springs as supplied by the manufacturer for each make of instrument in your department. The cost is minimal. Keep each separate brand in an envelope with the name of the instrument and make on the pack. They will come with flattened ends, ready for installation. All springs in a particular set will be usable in a specific instrument for which they were ordered, but they will *not* be marked to designate which key they are intended for. You will have to make the selection yourself.

Proper Selection and Installation: First, obtain the proper length, so that the spring will extend through the post to just beyond the spring hook (where the spring hooks on the key). Next, select the right spring diameter. The spring should enter the hole in the post (point first) and fit snugly enough so it will not wobble.

To install: With the key removed, force the flattened end in the hole with pliers (one jaw on the spring and the other jaw on the opposite side of the post). After the spring is wedged, it will be perpendicular to the post and will exert little force. To increase its force or strength, the spring must be bent very slowly with pliers. When a spring holds the key closed, such as low F$\sharp$, always bend the spring away from the tonehole. When a spring holds the key open, always bend the spring toward the tonehole.

Spring Too Long: If you have an assortment of needle springs and find one that fits the hole in the post but is too long, insert the spring into the hole and replace the key. Allow the tip of the spring to extend a minute distance beyond the spring hook. In this position, bend the opposite end of the spring (which extends from the back of the post) at the post, then retract the entire spring and clip at the bend. Rest the clipped end of the spring on your vise and flatten it with a bench hammer. Insert the spring into the post and secure it by placing one jaw of your pliers on the flattened end of the spring and the other jaw on the opposite side of the post. Squeeze until the spring is in place.

Replacing a flat spring also requires shortening the replacement; for best bearing surface, bend the end of the spring upward, as illustrated:

Fig. 7

Natural form   Bent spring

Spring Too Short: When the tip of a needle spring is broken off to where it is too short to reach the hook, *do not* try to drive out the remaining needle or you might break off the post. Clip the spring about ¹/₈ inch from the post; then take longnose pliers and place one jaw over the end of the spring and the other on the opposite side of the post and push the spring out. A fine pair of pliers, which has a slit in the center of one of the jaws, is available for this operation. It is also excellent for inserting new springs.

In driving out saxophone springs you can easily break off the posts or bend them to where the rods will no longer enter the posts. The best procedure is to clip the spring, as described above.

Flute Springs: Flute springs are usually made of a softer metal to fill the need for light action. When a spring breaks off, it usually occurs at the post. Since the part that remains in the post is hard to remove, it is strongly recommended that you leave flute spring replacement to your repairman.

Baritone Saxophone Springs: The flat-spring action of some baritone saxophones is not strong enough to hold the high F key closed. This may be remedied by placing a water key spring (with large coil) on the hinge.

*   *   *

Springs for saxophones, clarinets, and other woodwind instruments have changed through the years. Older saxophones had larger, softer, and less responsive springs—hence difficulty is encountered in replacing springs in such saxophones. When you find a spring of the modern type large enough to wedge into the spring hole of an older saxophone, it is usually so stiff that it causes the action to be heavy. Most repair shops have a supply of the older springs or can temper a spring to fit your needs.

Years ago, saxophone and clarinet springs were not tapered (like a needle); neither were they very responsive, because of their soft metal construction. Manufacturers then introduced a smaller tempered steel spring and tapered it to give a lighter and more resilient action. Now, with the improvement in metals, the straight spring is once again being used. It not only gives light, positive action, but is rust-resistant and can be bent to give more strength without the danger of breaking.

BRASS INSTRUMENT SPRINGS

The springs on the water keys of brass instruments are frequently made of steel. Since it is impossible to keep moisture off the spring when eliminating saliva, it is necessary to oil the springs periodically to prevent rusting and breakage. However, some manufacturers use brass or bronze springs since this metal will not rust. This type of spring tends to lose its strength, but it is easily restored by gripping the end of the spring (usually wrapped around the post) with pliers and pulling. This will tighten the coil around the key hinge and renew its strength. Wrap the end of the spring back around the post and clip off any excess.

This procedure may also be used to strengthen rotary valve springs (French horn).

Piston Valve Springs: Piston valve springs should be replaced with duplicates of the original spring. The stroke (distance the valve moves) is not the same on all makes of brass instruments, even though they are of the same type. If the spring is too short, it will cause a bounce at the top of the action and will not push the valve completely up. If the spring is too long, the valve can not be pushed completely to the bottom of the casing, thus preventing the ports of the valves and valve casings from meeting correctly.

Spring Too Short: In an emergency, a short spring can be stretched by pulling from both ends. But be careful not to disfigure the spring. A crooked spring will exert an uneven force when compressed, causing the spring to bulge and rub the side of the casing. The result is unsatisfactory valve action and unnecessary valve wear. For this reason, never stretch valve springs to make dirty valves work. Always keep the valves and casings clean.

Spring Too Long: Long springs may be shortened, *in an emergency*, by clipping off a section of the coil. This will also create the problem of unsatisfactory valve action and wear. Clipping the spring will not leave the bottom coil of the spring flat as it was originally, and uneven action will result.

4

CLARINET

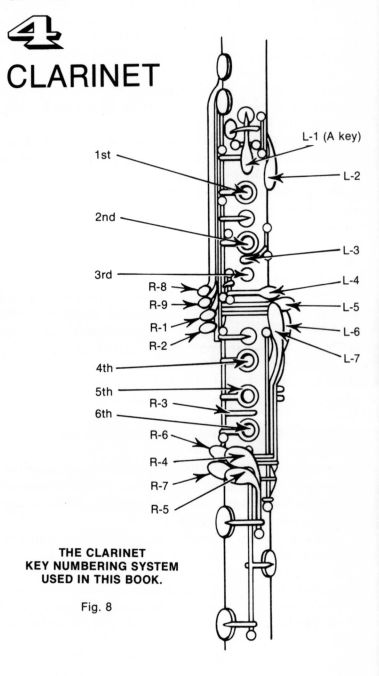

1st

2nd

3rd

R-8

R-9

R-1

R-2

4th

5th

R-3

6th

R-6

R-4

R-7

R-5

L-1 (A key)

L-2

L-3

L-4

L-5

L-6

L-7

**THE CLARINET
KEY NUMBERING SYSTEM
USED IN THIS BOOK.**

Fig. 8

16

GENERAL CARE

Wood clarinets require special attention, and the procedures described in this chapter are designed to insure that this instrument receives the care required for optimum performance. First, however, there are certain general recommendations, frequently overlooked, that should be followed. Adherence to these suggestions will eliminate more than 90 per cent of your repair problems.

■ Swab the wood clarinet after each playing. Although the wood used in a clarinet is soaked in oil for a long period prior to construction, saliva will draw out the oil, which must be replaced periodically.

Pour a small amount of bore oil on a wool swab as it is being rotated. Then wrap an absorbent rag around the swab and squeeze it lightly to absorb the surplus oil. If you fail to do this before pushing the swab through the clarinet, the surplus oil will run down through the toneholes and settle on the pads, causing their deterioration. (Note: Olive oil or sweet oil of almond, obtainable from any drugstore, may be used as an emergency substitute for bore oil.)

■ Oil movable parts. One way of oiling the key mechanism is with a small commercial hypodermic-type oiler, a procedure that eliminates mess and saves a lot of time. Apply oil to the rod ends at the pivot screws and hinge key posts. Also coat the springs with oil to prevent them from rusting and breaking.

Another method: dip a small watercolor brush in oil, then drag it across the top of the bottle to remove any excess oil. With the tip of the brush, oil the rod ends at the pivot screws and hinge key posts.

After oiling these movable parts, paint the springs to prevent them from rusting.

■ Use cork grease on the tenon corks to preserve the corks and prevent key damage. If the clarinet is difficult to assemble because of dry corks, do not grip the joints to force them together; this will only result in bent keys.

■ Various manufacturers of high-quality clarinets align the grain of the barrel with the grain on the body of the clarinet. They align the trademarks on the two sections accordingly, and therefore they suggest that the trademarks be aligned each time the instrument is assembled. The same principle applies to the bell.

■ The barrel on wood clarinets should always be removed after practicing. Caution students to follow this procedure. Otherwise, a clarinet may remain assembled at home for days at a time, and the moisture caused by saliva will expand the wood. When the student finally attempts to disassemble the instrument, he may find the top tenon swollen to such an extent that the barrel cannot be removed. This swollen condition also causes wood clarinets to crack.

■ A wood clarinet should not be subjected to extreme temperature changes. However, if the instrument is exposed to extremely cold weather, it should be left in its case at room temperature for a reasonable period before playing.

■ Oil all rods, screws, and springs immediately after cleaning an instrument with polish.

■ To avoid bent keys, students should never carry band books, folders, or similar materials in the instrument case. Periodic cleaning of the case is also essential to remove items that float around and cause clarinet malfunction.

PROBLEMS AND REPAIR PROCEDURES

Instrument repairmen are fortunate that clarinets are so similar, structurally and mechanically, and that they have remained so for generations. Indeed, a competent clarinet repairman of thirty years ago would be completely capable of performing expert work on today's clarinets.

Efficient clarinet repair, then, does not require knowledge of changing designs and systems (as, for example, in automobile mechanics). But it does demand definite and exact procedures (including diagnosis). For the clarinet is structurally complex and a great deal of care must be taken when handling this instrument.

The following procedures have been utilized extensively, with considerable success. Each clarinet malfunction has its own characteristic—or several distinguishing signs—which you will soon learn to recognize.

Consistent Squeak: A squeak (or unsatisfactory performance) is usually caused by one of the following:

1. Toneholes not covered completely.
2. Accidentally touching and opening a key.
3. Reed not sealed perfectly on the mouthpiece.
4. A mechanical leak or bad pads.

Locating leak: To find a leak, first check to see if the clarinet is cracked (providing it is a wood clarinet). Generally, a crack will appear near the top of the upper section, or between the joint ring and the first tonehole of the bottom section. If a crack occurs on the bottom section, it usually starts in the female part of the center joint. A crack may be difficult to see when the clarinet is disassembled; however, when the center joint is pushed over the light tenon cork of the upper section, the crack will open. The leak can be eliminated temporarily by binding it with cellulose tape, until the instrument can be taken to a repairman, who will apply a flush band or pin it.

Next, check the pads for a leak. The most widely used clarinet pads are bladder pads—constructed of felt with a cardboard back and covered with bladder skin. (See detailed section on clarinet pads, page 38.)

Intermittent Squeak: Frequently, a clarinet appears to be in satisfactory condition but squeaks intermittently. To locate the malfunction, check the following:

1. Look for a split reed or burr on the top mouthpiece rail.

To correct: Change the reed or *very* carefully file the burr down.

2. Check the adjustment screw on the A♭ (L-2) key. Open the key and, listening very closely, let it snap closed. A metallic click indicates that the A♭ adjustment screw (on top) is in too far, causing the A♭ key to hit the A key (L-1) rather than the tonehole. There should always be a tiny distance between these two keys and the only audible sound should be the soft thud of the pad hitting the tonehole.

To correct: If a metallic click is present, turn the screw in a counterclockwise direction until the click is no longer noticeable *(see photo 3)*. Next, test the clarinet. This minor adjustment will most likely eliminate the trouble. If a clarinet is not functioning properly, always check the A♭ adjustment screw first.

Photo 3

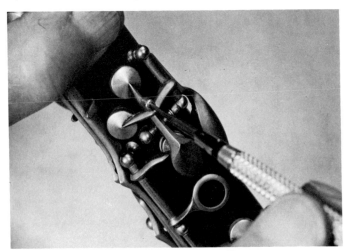

3. Check the throat A key (L-1). The throat A key may not be closing completely. It may appear to close properly, but if you allow it to return toward the tonehole very slowly, it will not close completely. If the key uses a flat spring, this may be caused by rust on the foot of the spring, which prevents it from sliding. If the surface on which the spring slides becomes dirty or rough, the spring will not function properly. Place a drop of oil or a bit of cork grease in the spring groove. If this procedure does not correct the problem, the spring tension is most likely incorrect.

To correct: Remove the key and bend the end of the spring down for increased strength. Note where to bend the spring (flat type) on the throat A key (L-1) to strengthen it:

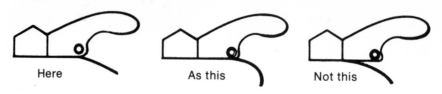

Here   As this   Not this

Fig. 9

If the A key (L-1) uses a needle spring, the spring must be bent away from the tonehole to exert more force, as shown in the following diagram:

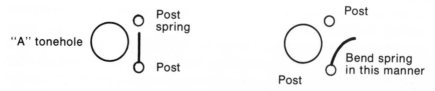

Fig. 10

4. Check the left-hand thumb-hole ring. This ring has an extension on the opposite side of the hinge (under the arch of keys R-8 and R-9, C and B side trill keys) that connects the first finger (left-hand) key to produce the note F. If keys R-8 and R-9 are bent down at the arch, one of the trill keys (usually key R-9, B trill) will raise just enough to make the clarinet squeak when the thumb ring is pressed.

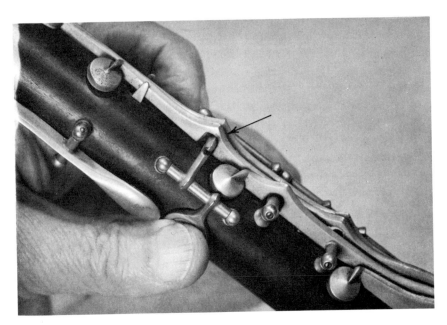

Photo 4

To correct: Place a screwdriver under the trill key, just to the side of the arch *(see arrow, photo 4)*, and press down on its pad cup. This will raise the arch to its original height and allow the thumb key to move naturally without touching the trill key.

5. It is also possible that the trill keys are not bent down at the arch, but the thumb ring may be bent up so high that when it is pressed it raises the straight trill key.

To correct: Remove the thumb ring and place it in a bench vise. Insert the hinge screw in the key so as not to spring or bend the tubing (hinge). Gently press the ring or lightly tap with your rawhide mallet until the ring is bent down. After placing the key back on the clarinet, you may find that the ring was bent too far; raise the ring with the end of your pad slick. To check the height of the thumb ring, depress the ring and see if it closes the first finger (left-hand) F key. If it does not, hold the entire first finger key down and bend down the back extension that fits over the thumb ring extension until the key closes. *(See Caution, pg. 45.)*

Buzz: The skin of a pad is loose and vibrating.

To correct: Replace the pad.

Warble: A warble is generally caused by a loose pad in the first finger F♯ (left-hand) key. This pad and its recessed tonehole are located directly beneath the foot of key L-1 (A key). The key is situated very close to the clarinet body and will not permit a loose pad to escape. Thus, if the pad is loose when the instrument is played, it will vibrate.

To correct: Merely affix the pad if it is relatively new, or replace it if it is an old pad. Weak springs will allow loose pads in closed keys to vibrate.

Airy Sound on Low C: If the pad at the top of the bottom ring section (stack) is too close to the tonehole, low C will have an airy quality. Reasons for the pad being too close to the tonehold are:

1. The cork on the foot of the bottom bridge key is too thick.

To correct: Place a strip of fine-grained sandpaper (grit up) under the bridge key cork. Apply slight tension to the key and withdraw the sandpaper. Repeat the procedure until enough cork has been removed to allow proper pad height for a clear tone.

2. The bridge key is bent down.

To correct: Straighten the bridge key with flatnose pliers.

3. Bottom bridge key is resting on the music lyre ring.

To correct: If the lyre ring is at fault, remove the ring and file it down until the bridge key does not contact it.

Vibration: Vibrations may be caused by the following:

1. One of the ligature screws is not tight.

To correct: Tighten the ligature screws.

2. Silencer skin is missing from end of key L-6 or L-7 (low F♯ and low E).

To correct: First, remove the key; moisten the tip of the key, then place it on the center of a new silencer skin. The skin will adhere sufficiently to reassemble the key. If you do not have silencer skins, use the skin from a small clarinet pad.

3. The ring on the bell is loose.

To correct: The loose ring should be tightened by a professional repairman.

Poor Tone Quality on Low A or 4th Space E: This is generally the result of key R-5 (low F–middle C) resting too closely to the tonehole, which may be caused by the following:

1. Pad is too thick or baggy.

To correct: Replace the pad with one of the correct thickness.

2. Key is bent.

To correct: Bend the key back to its original position with flatnose pliers, providing the key was not cast. If the key was cast, consult your repairman.

3. Cork on bottom of left-hand keys L-5, L-6, and L-7 is too thick or the piece of cork between keys L-5 and R-5 is too thick.

To correct: Place the grit side of a strip of fine-grained sandpaper (or emery cloth) against the cork and very carefully reduce the size of the cork.

4. Adjustment screw (where keys L-5 and R-5 meet) is in too far. (Not all clarinets have this adjustment screw.)

To correct: Turn the adjustment screw in a counterclockwise direction until the R-5 pad is in correct position.

Cannot Play Open G, A, or A♭: If the rest of the clarinet functions properly, check the spring to the first finger F♯ key. This spring is probably:

1. Unhooked.

To correct: Merely reposition the spring with your spring hook.

2. Broken.

To correct: The spring must be replaced. If the spring is broken off flush with the post, allow your repairman to extract the remaining spring. If a stub of the spring protrudes from the post, rest one jaw of needlenose pliers against the end of the protruding spring and the other jaw on the opposite side of the post (below the spring). Squeeze the pliers until the spring protrudes from the opposite side of the post, enough to withdraw completely with pliers.

Insert a spring that fits snugly into the hole; then replace the key. Allow the tip of the spring to extend a minute distance beyond the spring hook. In this position, bend the opposite end of the spring (which extends from the back of the post); then retract the entire spring and clip at the bend. Rest the clipped end of the spring on your vise and flatten it with a bench hammer. Insert the spring into the post and secure by placing one jaw of your needlenose pliers on the flattened end of the spring and the other jaw on the opposite side of the post. Squeeze until the spring is in place.

Cannot Play in Upper Register: Check the octave key port.

1. The accumulation of moisture in the vent will cause the pad to stick. Then, when the octave key is continually forced open, the pad skin will eventually tear loose, remaining on the vent opening. Even though the key is raised, the small portion of skin that is stuck to the vent blocks the tonehole.

To correct: Clean out the port and replace the pad with either cork or a new pad.

2. Small particles from the swab will collect inside the vent of the octave key port. If the accumulation becomes too large, the vent will be completely blocked.

To correct: Remove the octave key and clean it with a pipe cleaner. In an emergency, raise the octave key and blow through the octave key port or vent.

Cannot Play Low C: To locate malfunction:

1. Check key R-2 (side B♭ trill key). Key R-2 is located where it can easily be bent *(see photo 5)*. The pedal of this key may become bent to where it catches under key R-1—the key just above it. Consequently, key R-2 is prevented from closing completely.

Photo 5

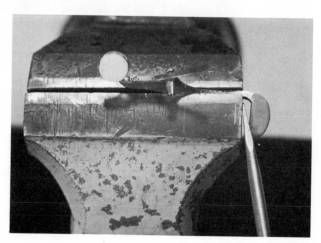

Photo 6

To correct: Key R-2 must be removed and straightened if it is to function properly. Place the key (upside down) in a bench vise and very carefully close the vise. The key should now be straightened. Place flatnose pliers or a large screwdriver between the pedal of the key (part touched by finger when playing) and the end of the vise, and move *slowly* away from the vise until the pedal is almost perpendicular to the key (*see photo 6*).

2. Check the spring on the side B♭ key (R-2). This spring has a tendency to slide out of the spring groove and under the edge of the G♯ (key L-4) key pad, thus holding key L-4 open just enough to permit leakage (*see photo 7*).

Photo 7

To correct: Push the spring back into its groove with the forked end of a spring hook.

3. Check the pad cup of key L-4 (G♯). The outer edge of the G♯ (key L-4) tonehole is recessed on most clarinets so the pad will not have to wrap around the body of the clarinet to cover the tonehole. The entire pad fits into this depression. If the key becomes bent either to the right or to the left, the pad or pad cup will ride on the edge of the recessed rim (*see photo 8*). In this position, the pad will not cover the tonehole.

Photo 8

To correct: Use flatnose pliers to grip the extension arm (not pad cup) and bend the key until the pad centers over the tonehole and enters the recessed area.

4. Check the spring on key L-1 (A). Be careful when replacing this (flat-type) spring. If the replacement spring is too long, the end will extend beyond the end of the spring groove and into or under the first finger F♯ key pad. If this occurs, the F♯ key pad will either be punctured or prevented from closing, with air leakage resulting.

To correct: Remove key L-1 (A) and clip the spring to the correct length (so it will not extend past the end of the spring groove when the key is closed). If the spring is bent up slightly at the very end, it will permit easier movement in the groove.

5. Check key L-3 (B♭-E♭). Key L-3 is subjected to a great deal of moisture from perspiring hands and, consequently, the hinge screw has a tendency to rust and bind the key. Gently press the key, allowing it to close slowly.

To correct: If the key remains open, oil the hinge screw. If the key still refuses to close, remove it in the proper manner and strengthen the spring (as described in Chapter 3).

6. Check the second finger (left-hand) key (used to play D). Press the ring to see if it is even (level) with the tonehole rim when the pad (in above cup) completely covers its tonehole (*see photo 9*).

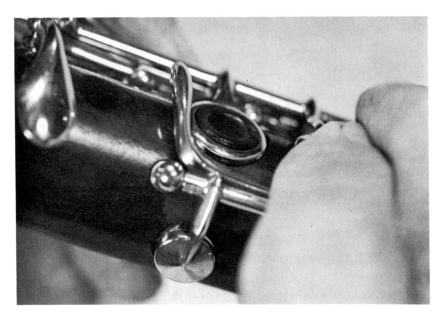

Photo 9

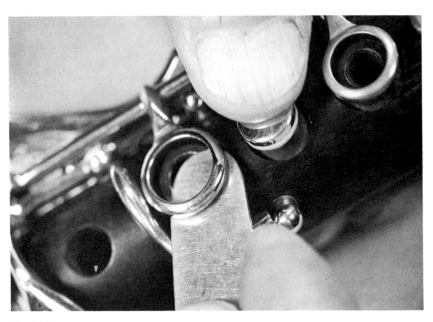

Photo 10

If the ring extends beyond the rim of the tonehole, the pad will not seat. The fingertip will rest on the tonehole rather than on the ring that seats the pad.

To correct: Place the small end of a pad slick between the ring and tonehole, then press the second finger pad cup (between the first and second finger rings). This will raise the second finger ring (*see photo 10*). *Be sure* the pad slick lies flat on the entire tonehole so that you do not chip the tonehole ridge. If you get the ring too high, reverse the procedure by placing the slick under the pad and pressing the ring.

7. Check key L-2 (throat A♭ key). The arm of key L-2 is constructed to arch over the A key (L-1) and extends above all other keys on the top joint. If the top of this key is hit accidentally, the arch will spread, pushing the pad cup to a point where it contacts key R-8 (side high C trill key). If this occurs, the A♭ key pad will not cover the tonehole completely and air leakage will result.

To correct: Key L-2 must be straightened to its original form. After placing the hinge screw in the key (so you won't bend or spring the hinge tubing), place the arm of the key upside down on the top corner of your bench vise. Using small pliers, bend the key toward the vise to restore its arch (*see photo 11*). If the A♭ key is bent only slightly, the air leak can be eliminated by replacing the pad with a smaller one.

Photo 11

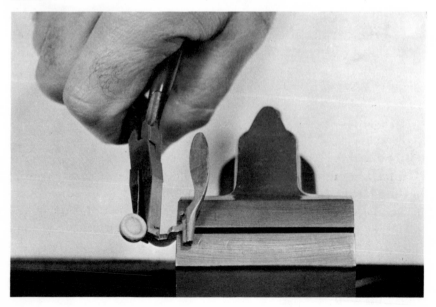

8. Check key L-2 (A♭) to see if it is holding open due to binding. This can be caused by the hinge screw in key L-1 (A) being in too far and contacting key L-2.

To correct: Adjust hinge screw.

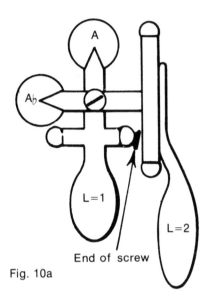

Fig. 10a

After checking all the probable causes of leaks, assemble the top half of the clarinet and play all possible notes. If you get a good, solid sound with the thumb and three fingers down (as in playing low C), there is no leak. If the clarinet still does not play satisfactorily when completely assembled, the trouble is in the bottom section.

Cannot Play Below Low C: To locate malfunction:

1. Check the bridge keys (keys extending from the top and bottom sections which overlap at the center tenon joint). With the clarinet assembled, cover the toneholes on the top section as if playing low D. Now finger or play low B♭. Did you feel any movement of the top keys when playing B♭? If you did, one of the bridge keys is bent and is not permitting the pad on the bottom stack to close. To find the bent part (top or bottom), hold the clarinet horizontally and look at the bridge keys. Both keys should be parallel to the clarinet body. This makes it relatively easy to locate the bent key.

To correct: Using flatnose pliers, straighten the faulty key so the pad just above the low B♭ ring will close. Be careful not to bend the key too far or first finger (both hands) B♭-E♭ will be affected. If the bottom key is bent up, be careful not to bend it down too much or it will not only interfere with first fingers B♭-E♭, but also lower the pad on the bottom stack, resulting in an airy low C.

2. Check key R-3 (F♯ auxiliary key). The pedal of key R-3 can become bent enough to touch the rod on the lower joint stack. While listening very closely, push the key down and let the pad snap shut. If you hear a metallic click, it is most likely caused by the pedal touching the stack rod. If this occurs, the pad cannot close properly. Check the R-3 pad with your leaklight (see pg. 43).

To correct: Place your left thumb on the pad cup (key R-3) and your right thumb on the pedal. Force the pedal down far enough so the pad will close and the pedal will not touch the rod.

3. Check the rings on the bottom stack. Each ring should be level (even) with its tonehole rim. Place your fingers on the outside rim of the rings; press and draw your fingers over the toneholes. If you feel the edges of the tonehole, the rings are too low. These rings must be absolutely even with the toneholes for a positive, instant response—especially when trilling. If the rings extend past or below the tonehole rims, the pads will not seat, since the fingertips rest on the toneholes rather than on the ring which seats the pad.

Photo 12

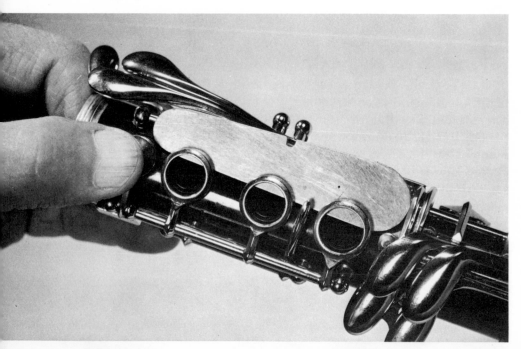

To correct: Place the entire length of pad slick under all three rings (covering at least one third of each tonehole to prevent chipping). With your thumb, press down on the pad cup at the top of the stack (*see photo 12*). This will raise all three rings equally. If the rings become too high, reverse the procedure by placing the slick under the pad; then press all three rings simultaneously. If the rings are too high, your fingers will rest on the rings rather than on the toneholes.

4. Check each post to see that it is not turned. Most of the keys on the bottom section have pivot screws to hold the keys in place. All key rods must be straight or perpendicular to the post surface for keys to work properly and pad cups to center over their toneholes. Pivot screws must enter key rods straight, as indicated:

Fig. 11

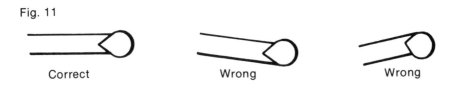

Correct   Wrong   Wrong

If a post is turned, it will move the rod in the same direction, causing the pad cup on the affected key to cover the tonehole insufficiently, impairing mechanical action.

To correct: Grip the post with pliers and return it to its original position. If the turned post happens to be a spring post, the spring tension will most likely become so great that, rather than pushing the key up, the tension will move the post back. If this should occur, remove the key, back-screw the post about halfway, and apply a post shim (commercially available). If post shims are not available, place a very small amount of pumice in the hole around the screw and then tighten the post to its original position. If you do not have pumice, a good substitute is the abrasive from fine-grained sandpaper. This usually solves the problem, but if the post still turns freely take the instrument to your repairman. He will either rebush the post hole or post, or anchor the post with epoxy.

Little Finger Key Alignment: Keys used by the little fingers (L-5, L-6, L-7, R-4, R-5, R-6, R-7) should be checked regularly for

Fig. 12

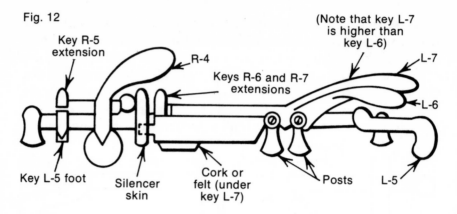

Key R-5 extension

R-4

(Note that key L-7 is higher than key L-6)

L-7

Keys R-6 and R-7 extensions

L-6

Key L-5 foot

Silencer skin

Cork or felt (under key L-7)

Posts

L-5

correct alignment. There must not be any play (lost motion) between their connecting parts. These keys must not be bent if the result impairs any mechanical action. *Remember:* Do not bend keys that have embossed numbers on them.

1. Check keys L-6 and L-7 to see that they are straight and do not come in contact with each other. Key L-7 should be higher than key L-6 so the student will not touch key L-6 when using key L-7. Correct alignment is illustrated here:

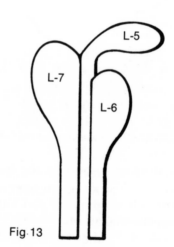

L-5

L-7

L-6

Fig. 13

2. Check the posts at either end of key L-5. If either post turns, it will cause key L-5 to bind with the extensions of keys R-6 and R-7.

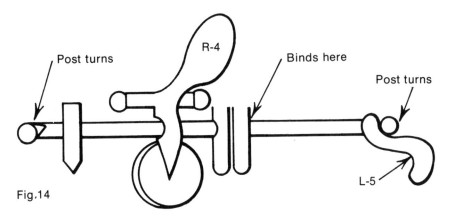

Fig.14

To correct: Grip the post with pliers and return it to its original position.

3. Check the end of key L-6 if you are unable to play the low notes. Some clarinets have an arch at this point; if the key is bent out it rides on the tip of the arch and holds key R-6 open.

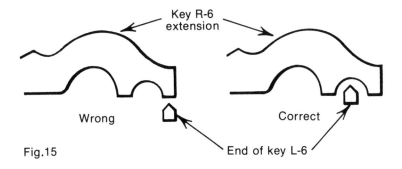

Fig.15

To correct: Use flatnose pliers to bend key L-6 in until it enters the arch.

4. Check the crowsfoot extension on the R-5 key (low F) and listen very carefully as you close it. If you hear a click as you close the key, rather than the soft thud of the pad hitting the tonehole, the crowsfoot is hitting the clarinet body and not permitting the pad to close.

To correct: Push down on the pad cup and up on key pedal R-5 until the pad closes and the click disappears.

5. Check the crowsfoot extension of key R-5 to be sure it is covered with cork.

6. Check alignment of keys R-4, R-5, R-6, and R-7.

To produce low E, whether using L-7 or R-7 singly, key R-7 must contact the crowsfoot extension of key R-5 and close the key. The same is true in playing low F♯ with either key L-6 or R-6. One reason the Boehm system replaced the Albert system was because it allowed these notes to be played singly with either hand. These keys are out of adjustment rather frequently, however, so many instructors prefer that their students use both keys L-7 and R-5 when playing low E.

For correct alignment, the four keys used by the little finger of the right hand should be as illustrated:

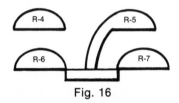

Fig. 16

The most frequently encountered problems of alignment are these:

a. Key R-7 does not contact the crowsfoot of key R-5.

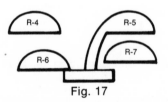

Fig. 17

To correct: First check the bottom end of key L-7 to see if the cork or felt is missing. If it is, replace the missing material. If not, key L-7 is bent. With pliers or large screw-driver, secure the end of the key L-7 extension opposite the pedal (on the other side of the post); then press the key

L-7 pedal with your thumb until it contacts the crowsfoot.
b.   Keys R-6 and R-7 are not touching the crowsfoot.

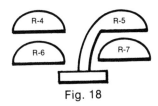

Fig. 18

To correct: First check the crowsfoot. If it is bent down, place one jaw of your pliers on the top of key R-5 and the other jaw under the crowsfoot. Press until the crowsfoot contacts both keys R-6 and R-7.

Other possible causes of the problem: (1) the felt or cork is missing from under left-hand keys L-7 and L-6; (2) the connecting arms from keys R-6 and R-7 to keys L-7 and L-6 are bent upward.

To correct: (1) Replace the cork or felt under the ends of keys L-7 and L-6 with material thick enough to lower keys R-6 and R-7 to the crowsfoot. (2) To straighten the connecting arms, bend pedals R-6 and R-7 down simultaneously until both keys are lowered enough to directly contact the crowsfoot.

c.   Key R-6 is pulling down on key R-5, causing lost motion between the crowsfoot and key R-7. This also forces the key R-5 pad too close to its tonehole, producing a distorted tone quality on low A.

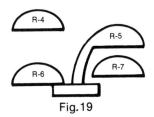

Fig.19

To correct: Check the pad in key R-6. If it is too thick, replace it with a thinner pad. Next check key R-6. If it is bent down, use your thumb or a flatnose pliers to push up on the key R-6 pedal until the crowsfoot contacts key R-7.

d. Key R-6 is not contacting the crowsfoot.

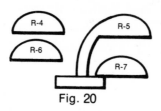

Fig. 20

To correct: Check the pad in key R-6. If it is too thin, replace it with a thicker pad. Next check key R-6. If it is bent up, place pliers or screwdriver on the extension of key L-6 (opposite pedal); then, while applying pressure to the extension, press key R-6 with your thumb.

e. Key R-5 is lower than key R-4 and the crowsfoot is below both keys R-6 and R-7.

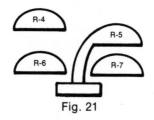

Fig. 21

To correct: Check to see if the cork is too thick either on the extension on the back of key R-5 (that contacts key L-5) or on the foot of key L-5 (low F). If so, replace with thinner cork. If key R-5 has an adjustment screw, check to see if it is in too far.

7. Check the low F and E pads to see that they are the correct distance from the toneholes. Using a feeler gauge, blowing test, or leaklight, check to see if the pads on both keys L-7 and R-7 are completely closed. If light emits from the F pad while the height of the E pad is correct, hold key R-5 and bend its pad cup down. If light emits from the E pad, bend the F pad cup up. It might be necessary to bend the E key down to prevent the F pad cup from

becoming too high. This will also prevent the crowsfoot from hitting the clarinet body.

If the clarinet still does not play satisfactorily after you have checked all the places indicated for leaks and malfunctions, try another mouthpiece and reed. With a little experience acquired by finding and correcting the "faults" described above, you should be able to detect malfunctions more readily through their general characteristics.

Additional Notes:

Silencer Skins: When installing silencer skins at the ends of keys L-7 and L-6 (keys must be removed), moisten the tip of the key, then place it on the center of the skin. The skin will adhere enough to replace the key in its correct position.

Pivot Screws: Before removing clarinet, saxophone, or flute pivot screws, first check to see if there is a pivot-lock screw in the side of the post. This screw must be withdrawn before the pivot screw can be moved.

Fig. 22

ALTO AND BASS CLARINETS

The key mechanisms of the alto and bass clarinets are very similar to the key mechanism of the soprano clarinet; however, the plateau system (pads rather than rings) is most prevalent.

To check for pad leaks insert a leaklight inside the instrument and—starting at the top—proceed to the bottom, stopping at each pad to see if light is emitted between the pad and the tonehole.

A pad that frequently hinders performance is on the low C key (third finger, left hand), which works in combination with the two keys just above it. To save time, check the low C pad first.

Other pads that may cause considerable trouble are the thumb and low G♯ key pads.

The bass clarinet octave key controls two pads; one must close when the other opens. The thumb key works in combination with the octave key. When the octave key pedal is pressed, the bottom octave key pad opens and when the thumb key is pressed, the bottom key pad closes and the top octave key pad opens. An adjustment screw regulates this action. If the bottom octave key does not close, turn the screw in a clockwise direction. If the octave key pads close but the thumb key will not, the adjustment screw is in too far.

Another reason why the thumb key will not close: either the extension in back of the first finger (F♯)—which contacts the extension from the thumb key—may be bent down, or the thumb key may be bent up. To correct this condition, refer to the same malfunction in the soprano clarinet section.

The low G♯ key pad must be checked and replaced more often than other pads because of its accessibility to saliva.

Also check the A♭ adjustment screw, bridge key, side B♭ pedal and others, as described in the soprano clarinet section.

Remember that the upper register and above on a bass clarinet (G—three fingers left hand) cannot be played without relaxing the embouchure.

BASSOONS, CONTRA-BASS CLARINETS, AND SARRUSOPHONES

These instruments are so complex and delicate that all repairs should be performed by a competent, professional repairman.

CLARINET PADS

A large percentage of necessary classroom repairs may very well be due to pad deficiencies. There are varieties of pads, pad cups and actions. To obtain maximum performance, including proper intonation and tone-production, the right materials must be used and correct installation procedures followed. A large number of clarinets enter the repair shop because the pad or pads replaced by the band director were the incorrect size or type.

To understand better the construction and composition of bladder pads (which are constructed of felt with a cardboard back and covered with a bladder skin), take one apart and examine it. Note that the skin is very thin and pliable; however, its texture is such that it makes the pad airtight. The felt is porous and when the skin is missing, broken, or cut, the pad leaks. The felt gives the pad body and is soft enough to receive the tonehole imprint.

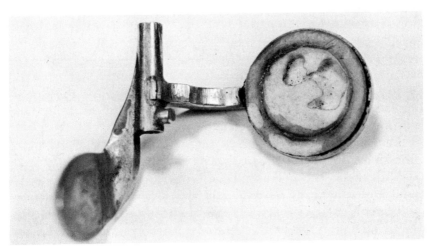

Photo 13

The inside of the pad is made of wool, and if a tiny hole appears in the center of a pad, there is a good possibility that the hole was caused by a moth (*see photo 13*). Clarinets that have been stored for even a short period of time may show evidence of the presence of moths. If you find pads with moth holes, replace the pads and have the student spray his case with a moth repellent. Remember: any time the pad skin is torn or punctured it will leak. If there are no holes, the skin is not broken or missing, and the pads seem to be in good condition, check to see if the pads are seated properly.

Each manufacturer of woodwind instruments has its own idea concerning the best materials for its particular product, and you will obtain optimum results if you use the same type of pad as was originally installed. It would definitely simplify matters if only one type of pad were needed. However, this is not possible, since manufacturers change their products and materials, students move in from other schools, and band directors change instrument models in accordance with their preferences. This means that most schools have a variety of instrument makes and models, which necessitates a knowledge of pads and pad installation.

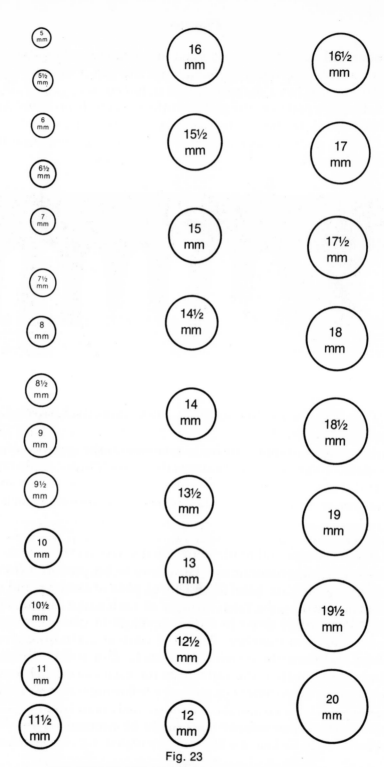

Fig. 23

PAD SIZE CHART (ALL SIZES IN MILLIMETERS).
WITH PAD FACE DOWN,
LOCATE CIRCLE WITH EQUAL DIAMETER.

Sizes: All clarinet pads are sized in millimeters. The sizes are determined by the width or diameter of the pad. Example: a size 10 clarinet pad has a diameter of 10 millimeters.

Selecting a pad to fit the pad cup offers very little problem. Any difficulties will be due to the thickness or type of pad used.

Clarinet pads are available in whole and half sizes, from 6½ to 20 millimeters.

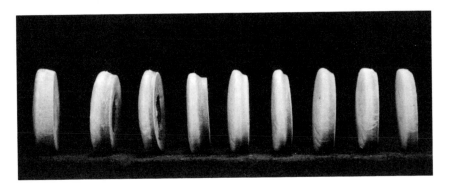

Photo 14

Pads may also be thin, medium, thick, extra-thick, beveled, or straight (*see photo 14*).

It is not uncommon to find variations in the same type and size pads. To repad clarinets correctly, repair shops usually carry several types of clarinet pads or many of each size in one style. Teachers or band directors do not need the variety of pads illustrated on the chart, since many of these sizes and types may never be used.

Most instrumental music departments have a certain make of clarinet that is predominant. However, to be prepared for an emergency, have on hand a few sets of pads of the type and size originally used by the manufacturer of each make clarinet. The pads will probably arrive in a small envelope or plastic container. *Do not* mix them together. Write the clarinet make on each envelope and keep the envelopes in stock. This will be the most efficient way to have the right pads for each clarinet. However, if you want an assortment of pads, the following sizes will be most beneficial. (Italicized numbers indicate pads most often replaced on clarinets. A few smaller pads might be necessary if you have clarinets with forked E♭-B♭—or articulated G♯—mechanisms.)

In medium pads with slight bevel:
   Sizes: 8, 9, *9½, 10,* 10½, *12,* 15, *16½, 17,* 17½
In thick pads:
   Sizes: 9, *10, 12,* 15½, *16½, 17,* 17½
In beveled pads:
   Sizes: 9, *10,* 11½, *12,* 16½, *17,* 17½

If you have an assortment of pads, compose a chart which indicates the make of instrument and the size pad required by each key. This takes time to work up, but it is time well spent if a pad must be quickly replaced.

The chart might read as follows:

Instrument	Pad Type	Thickness	F♯	A (etc.)	G♯	(Bot. St.)	F♯ Aux.	A♭	F-F♯-E
(Name)	S. Bev.	Med.	8½	10	9½	12	12	15½	16½
(Name)	Straight	Thick	9	9½	9½	12	12	16½	16½
(Name)	Beveled	Med.	10	10	10	12	12	17½	17½

S. Bev. means slight bevel; *A (etc.)* is for A, A♭, octave and side trill keys which usually use the same size pad; *Bot. St.* means bottom stack, which is the pad at the top of the bottom rings; the low F, F♯ and E keys usually use the same size pad. *(The example shown above is for no particular clarinet, but merely illustrates the pad listings.)*

To find the size and type of pad needed, fit each pad cup and then record it on the chart. Preparation of this chart will simplify fitting and ordering pads. Eventually, the need for the chart will diminish as you become familiar with each make clarinet and its characteristic pads.

You will find, as noted, variations in the same make of pads. On a beveled pad, the cardboard back should be centered in this way:

Fig. 24

Occasionally, the manufacturer errs and the cardboard back rests on one side, such as this:

Fig. 25

Do not use a pad of this kind, since it will not center correctly in the pad cup and therefore will not cover the tonehole satisfactorily.

Pads might also look like this:

Fig. 26

These lopsided pads are very difficult to seat. To do good work you must use good materials.

Checking Pad Seating:*

1. *Leaklight:* A woodwind leaklight is a convenient tool for locating leaks due to improper pad seating. Insert the light into the body of the clarinet, stopping directly under each tonehole and then closing the key. If a bright light appears between the pad and the tonehole, a leak is present.

2. *Vacuum and Blowing Test:* Some repairmen and instructors prefer to check pad seatings through the vacuum and blowing test for each section. Plug the end joint of each section with your hand (or preferably with a cork, leaving one hand free to find the leak) and cover the toneholes with the fingers of the other hand. Inhaling and producing a vacuum will quickly indicate if the leak is in that section. Blowing into the section will quickly indicate which pad is leaking.

3. *Feeler Gauge:* Use a feeler gauge (cellophane strip attached to a piece of wood, such as a wooden match or an old clarinet reed) to check the pads. Insert the cellophane between the pad and

---

* Although the three techniques commonly used are explained here, the author strongly recommends the leaklight as the most effective method.

tonehole; depress the key, then withdraw the gauge. A leak can be determined through easy slippage of the gauge.

If a pad becomes watersoaked it will usually harden, permitting leakage. In this case, the pad must be replaced.

If a pad is uneven or not centered in the pad cup it will not be level with the tonehole, causing leakage.

If the pad is in correct position in the pad cup, but air is still escaping, these are other possible causes: the key is bent; the pad is too thick; or the pad is too thin.

Adjusting Pads: First check the pads to see if they are level in the pad cups. If they are not, heat each pad cup quickly with a non-carbonous flame until the cement or shellac becomes soft. Then, lay the pad slick flat against the pad and move the pad until it is even or level with the cup *(see photo 15)* . If air is escaping from

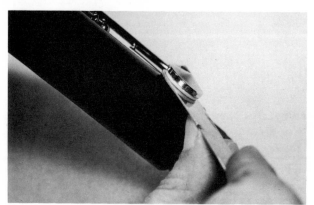

Photo 15

the back of the pad, push the pad inward with the pad slick, thus lowering it in back (towards tonehole). If air is escaping from the front, reverse the procedure and push the pad outward. *(An "old" pad should not be shifted, since the old seat may not align itself properly with the tonehole.)*

If the pad is level in the pad cup but light emits when the key is closed, one of the following may be the cause:

1. Pad is too thick (causing back of the pad to contact the tonehole first, thus permitting air leakage in front).

To correct: Check to see that all cement and cardboard backs have been removed from the pad cup. (This accumulation of materials adds unnecessary height to a pad.) If bits of materials remain in the cup, heat the cup and remove them. Removing this material might possibly solve the problem. If not, a thinner pad will most likely be necessary.

2. Pad is too thin (causing front of pad to touch tonehole first, permitting air leakage in back).

To correct: Use a thicker pad. If you do not have a thicker pad but do have French cement, remove the key and partially fill the cup with the cement. If you lack a thicker pad and cement, affix a layer of adhesive tape (not cellulose) to the bottom of the pad; then trim it to the exact size of the pad. Use as many layers as necessary to raise the pad to the correct thickness; then apply shellac to the back of the pad and place pad back in the cup.

3. Key is bent so pad cup is not level with the tonehole.

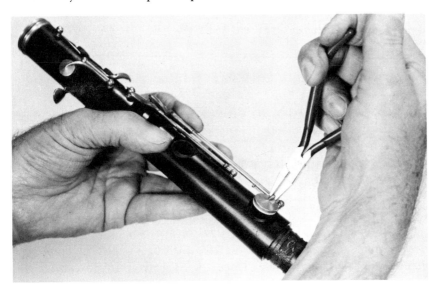

Photo 16

To correct: Very delicately, bend the arm of the key with pliers —toward the side where air is escaping—making sure the pad cup is level with the tonehole (*see photo 16*).

Caution! Some older clarinet keys are made of a material that will break more readily than bend. Therefore, *before you try to bend a key*, check to see if the key has an embossed number. If such a number exists, it was embossed on the key when it was cast. If this type of key breaks it cannot be brazed, so *do not* attempt to bend it. Heat will disintegrate the composition material of a cast key or cause it to drip like a candle. If a cast key is broken, it must be replaced. Supply the manufacturer with the original key number for proper replacement.

Do not apply the flame from a propane torch to this type of pad cup to seat the pad.

German silver keys are bendable and if broken can easily be brazed. If light emits from the side of a pad and you can see that it is caused by a bent key, straighten the key as described above. If the pad is the correct thickness and is centered level in the cup, but air still escapes from the front or back, straightening the key to overcome air-leakage is strictly a job for your repairman. The leak can be eliminated temporarily by shifting the pad in the cup.

Pad Installation:

Adhesive: Shellac or French cement, which is waterproof, provides a convenient adhesive for installing pads. Never use glue or mucilage since they are water-soluble. Moisture from saliva or condensation of breath will soften the glue, permitting the pad to move or drop out.

Tube shellac is probably the easiest adhesive to use. If you use a large amount of adhesive and find the tube too expensive or messy, you can mix your own by dissolving flake shellac in denatured alcohol. Keep the adhesive in an airtight container (empty cold cream or cream shampoo jar) to prevent the alcohol from evaporating. If it does evaporate, merely add additional alcohol and it will become usable again.

French cement, like sealing wax, requires heat. It is not necessary to use heat with liquid shellac, although many repair shops apply heat to evaporate the alcohol, thus seating the pads instantly. If heat is used to install a pad, prick the rim of the pad with a pin or needle spring. If the pad is completely sealed, heat will expand the air inside the pad, thus causing the pad to bulge or swell, preventing it from seating. The hole will permit expanded air to escape.

Pad slick: To install pads correctly, it is necessary to use a pad slick, as shown here:

Fig. 27

This permits you to straighten the pad while it is in the cup, or bind the center of the pad while the key is on the clarinet.

Replacing Lost or Defective Pads: To replace a lost or defective pad, be sure all of the old pad and adhesive are removed from inside the pad cup. (A size 58 needle spring is an excellent tool for removing old pads.) Select a pad of correct size and thickness; place it in the cup; then close the key to see if it fits. Next, remove the pad, apply shellac to the back of the pad; then place it back in its cup. Lay the pad slick flat against the pad and make sure the pad is evenly contained in the cup (*see photo 17*). Remove the slick and

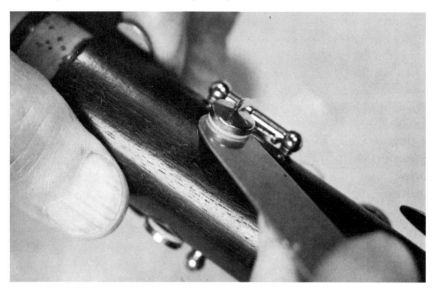

Photo 17

press firmly on the cup, forcing the pad down on the tonehole; hold for a second or two. Raise the key and check the tonehole imprint on the pad. If the pad is seated correctly, the imprint will have the same depression throughout the entire circumference of the pad. If it is deep on one side and shallow on the other, the pad is either not straight in the cup or the key is bent.

Replacing Large Pads: Use the same procedure for larger pads (low G♯, F, F♯, and E) as for small pads, *with this exception:* heat the pad cup and with the small end of the slick push up in the center of the pad and hold momentarily (*see photo 18*). This will bind the center of the pad in the concave pad cup and provide a flat surface for the pad to cover the tonehole. It will also eliminate the bulge or bag in the pad, which hinders resonance.

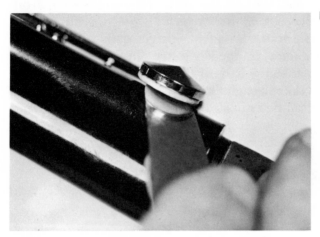

Photo 18

Never use a pad that is too thick or too large—the result will be a deep seat (impression of the tonehole on the pad). The roll formed around the pad cup will rest on the tonehole shoulder, preventing the tonehole from being properly covered. It may also protrude into the tonehole. To get a responsive, resonant tone, the pad should be the right size and thickness, with minimum seat.

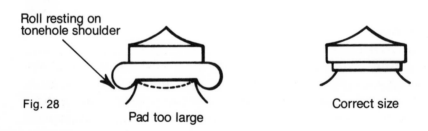

Roll resting on
tonehole shoulder

Fig. 28

Pad too large

Correct size

If you insert a light behind a pad that has a roll, you will see a thin circle of light where the pad touches the tip of the tonehole. This small leak, along with the bulge of the pad into the tonehole, will hinder resonance and prevent positive tone production—especially when trilling this key.

Installing Thick Pads: If you use a thick pad which has a hole in the back, apply shellac to the hole. Heat the pad cup momentarily; place the pad in the cup; then apply pressure to the center of the pad with the small end of the slick. This will bind the felt to the pad cup so the pad will not bulge or bag. Close the key and press firmly against the tonehole.

Installing Beveled Pads: If you use a beveled pad for a shallow cup, select one that fits into the cup so the rim of the cup rests on the outside of the pad. Apply shellac to the back of the pad; place the large end of the slick against the pad and straighten the pad. Remove the slick and close the key, pressing firmly against the tonehole. Check to see that the imprint is correct. To use a beveled pad, the tonehole shoulder must be large enough to receive the protruding part of the pad.

If the imprint on the pad is not correct (complete circle all around the pad), heat the cup momentarily; then lay the flat end of the slick against the pad and tilt it towards the side of the vague imprint. Hold for a second or so until the adhesive sets; then repeat the pressing procedure.

Use a light to see if the pad is seated correctly. If light emits from the back, reheat the cup to soften the adhesive. Lay the slick flat against the pad and push the pad towards the back. If the pad is leaking in front, reverse the procedure. With a little practice, you will learn just how much to move the pad to get the desired results.

If you are unable to close the leak in back of the key by this procedure, the pad is most likely too thin; if you cannot close the leak in front, the pad is most likely too thick.

Installing Low F♯ Pads (Key L-6–R-6): For several reasons, the most difficult pad to install in a clarinet is in key L-6–R-6 (low F♯). If the pad used is too thick, the right low F♯ pedal will push down on the crowsfoot extension of the low F key and lower the pad too close to its tonehole. This not only makes low A sound stuffy, but will disturb the action on keys L-7–R-7 (low E). If the pad is too thin, the extension opposite the pedal (on opposite side of the post), which permits use of left-hand key L-6, will touch the body of the clarinet before the pad touches the tonehole. If a light is used to check the seat of the low F♯ pad and light is visible around the entire pad, look at the end of key L-6 to see if it is resting on the body of the clarinet.

To correct: Use a thicker pad. If the replacement pad is exactly the same as the original pad you will not have any problem, although it might require shifting.

"Floating In" Pads: Various high-quality clarinets use pad cement for slight pad pivots; some use the cement just for the adhesive or to fill the concave cup so the pad will adhere to a flat surface. Clarinets with such key construction, requiring pads to be "floated in," are not uncommon. To float in pads, first remove the key, and then fill the pad cups with French cement (which will raise the height of the pad in the cup). Then heat the pad cup slightly and press down lightly on the tonehole. The soft cement permits the pad to pivot in the cup to position itself level with the tonehole, even though the key may not be level. If you have such a key-structured clarinet with a lost or worn pad, it is best not to disturb the cement. Try to find a pad of the same thickness and design as the one removed. First, puncture the side of the pad; apply shellac to the back of the pad; then, fit it in the cup.

Floating in pads takes much precision and experience in order to know just how much cement and heat to apply to the pad cup. With insufficient cement, the pad will not be high enough; with excess cement, the pad will be too high. If the pad cup is heated excessively, the cement will become too soft and will be forced out from under the pad when the cup is pressed to seat the pad.

CORKING CLARINET TENON JOINTS

The easiest and best way to replace clarinet tenon joint corks is to have strips of cork precut to the right size, with opposite ends tapered, as indicated:

Fig. 29

(If pre-cut strips cannot be obtained, see measuring and cutting procedure at end of this section.)

When the cork is wrapped around the tenon, the ends will overlap—as indicated:

Fig. 30

Attaching Cork Strips: Three recommended choices for adhesives are:

1. *Contact cement:* Apply contact cement to the tenon groove and to the back of cork. Let cement set for a few seconds until tacky, then wrap the cork around the tenon and hold a few seconds longer, until it adheres.

2. *Liquid shellac:* Apply liquid shellac to the tenon groove and back of the cork strip. Wrap the cork around the tenon and secure in place by wrapping a rubber band around it. Let it set overnight to dry.

3. *Stick shellac:*

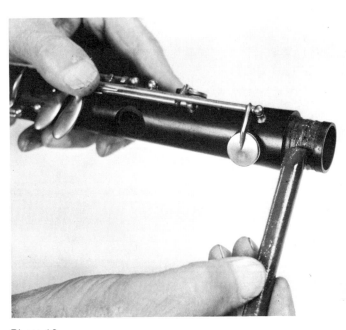

Photo 19

a. Hold the stick in a flame until soft, then deposit bits of shellac around the tenon (*see photo 19*).

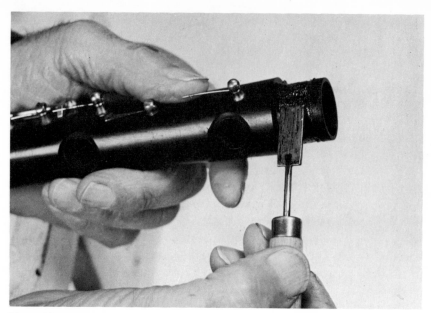

Photo 20

b. Hold the shellac iron in the flame until hot; then smooth out the shellac spots to cover all of the grooves (*see photo 20*). See that the shellac is a little thicker in one spot.

Photo 21

c. Hold this spot of thicker shellac close to your flame until the shellac becomes soft (*see photo 21*). Do not allow the flame to touch the clarinet.

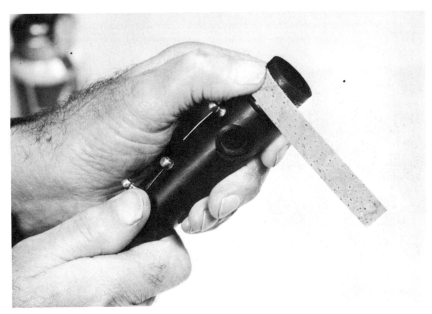

Photo 22

d. Place the tapered (down) end of the cork on the larger deposit of shellac and flatten the cork on the tenon grooves with your thumb (*see photo 22*).

Photo 23

e. Now, use the iron to soften the shellac as you ease around the tenon, each time pressing the cork in the groove (*see photo 23*).

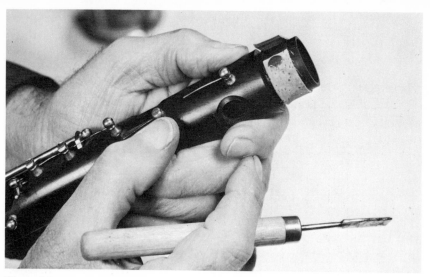

Photo 24

f.   Stop about ½ inch from the lap. Put a drop of shellac on
the lap and continue heating the rest of the shellac with
your iron, including the drop on the lap (*see photo 24*).

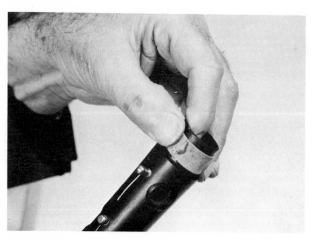

Photo 25

g.   Now, press the lap together (*see photo 25*).

After the cork is on the clarinet and the adhesive is set, use a
cork knife or single-edge razor blade to taper the edges, as indicated:

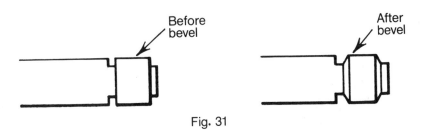

Fig. 31

The cork must fit snugly so that the tenon joint is secure; if you use the right cork thickness and apply cork grease, it should be a perfect fit. If the cork is too thick, use a strip of fine sandpaper to remove the excess cork. Be careful not to drag the sandpaper over the end of the tenon, since rounding off the edge of the tenon will loosen the joint.

Measuring and Cutting Cork Strips: If you are unable to obtain precut strips (some repair shops will prepare them for you), use a sheet of cork (obtainable in 4 x 12 inches) $1/16$ inch thick (some joints might require thicker). Span the tenon groove with the sheet of cork and the mark the needed width. Using a ruler and straightedge, cut the strips. The approximate length for each tenon is:

Mouthpiece	3 inches	$7/16$-inch wide
Top tenon	3 $1/8$ inches	$7/16$-inch wide
Center tenon	3 inches	$7/16$-inch wide
Bottom tenon	3 $1/2$ inches	$1/2$-inch wide

After cutting the strips, taper the ends—as previously illustrated—with a single-edge razor blade or knife; drag the end over fine-grade sandpaper or a fine-grade emery wheel.

If the cork is exposed to arid conditions it will become brittle and break when bent around the tenon. To make the cork pliable, either dampen it or place the cork in a smooth-jaw vise and then press.

Apply contact cement or stick shellac to the back of each strip of cork and allow to dry. Now the strips are ready for instant application.

After replacing a few tenon corks, you should find this operation effortless.

CLARINET QUICK-CHECK ROUTINE

1. See if any pads are missing.
2. See if any springs are unhooked.
3. Check the A♭ adjustment screw (key L-2).
4. Check the bridge key.
5. Check the side B♭ trill key pedal (R-2).
6. Check the throat A key (L-1).
7. Check the G♯ key pad cup (L-4).
8. Check side C and B trill keys (R-8 and R-9) arch and thumb-hole ring extension.
9. Check spring of side B♭ trill key (R-2).
10. Check key L-3 (B♭-E♭).
11. Check F♯ auxiliary key R-3 (bottom section).
12. Check crowsfoot on key R-5 (bottom section).
13. Look for crack.
14. Check pads with a leaklight.
15. Check mouthpiece tip for chips.

CHAPTER

FLUTE

Flutes are more difficult than clarinets to repair primarily because the keys work in combination and the pads require more skill and patience to install. Also, the springs on older flutes are quite soft and difficult to adjust for the right tension needed to obtain the desired key action.

Many students continue to play flutes when various tones lose their resonance. The pitch may be accurate, but the tone is not resonant or vibrant. This is what is meant when it is stated that the flute is not producing to its maximum. Slight malfunctions may go unnoticed by students; however, there is one specific note that both students and director do notice: B♭ (tuning note). Therefore, many flutes enter repair shops because this one important note is not functioning properly, which in turn reveals that other tones are also defective. If the flute section does not sound at its peak, this does not necessarily mean that the students are not practicing. Mechanical malfunctions may very well be the cause.

CHECKPOINTS AND REPAIR PROCEDURES

1. Check to see if any of the springs are unhooked.
2. Check to see if any of the wedge pins (the small steel part extending through the stack rod) are missing.
3. Check the long rod that goes through the first finger key. If the flute has not been oiled, this rod will work loose and back

out far enough so the tip that forms a pivot and holds the second finger key in place will not function properly. Consequently, the pads in the second finger keys will not cover the toneholes. This is the most common reason for not being able to obtain first finger B♭.

Photo 26

To correct: Using a small screwdriver, turn the screw back in until the second finger key is anchored (*see photo 26*). Some flutes have a lock screw in the second post which prevents the screw from moving.

4. Check the G♯ key. If the pedal becomes bent to the point where it touches the G key, when the G key is closed, the G♯ key will open just enough to cause leakage.

Photo 27

To correct: Gently bend the pedal back to its original position (*see photo 27*).

5. Check the G♯ key pad to see if air is escaping. When the flute is placed in some types of cases, it rests on the G♯ key cup. When these cases are accidentally dropped, the G♯ key cup receives the blow (usually hitting on the front of the cup and pushing it up in the back, permitting leakage). This can also occur by setting the case down too hard. The same thing happens to the E♭ key on the foot joint.

To correct: Gently lift up on the front of the G♯ key pad cup.

6. Use a leaklight to check pads for leakage. There are four keys that have adjustment screws, and by manipulating these screws you can raise or lower the keys on the stack. For example: when closing the second finger key (A) two keys close. Using your leaklight, check if both keys are closing sufficiently. If light is emitting from the top key, turn the adjustment screw to the right with a small screwdriver until no bright light is visible (*see photo 28*). If you see a faint glow through the porous pad, it is seated cor-

Photo 28

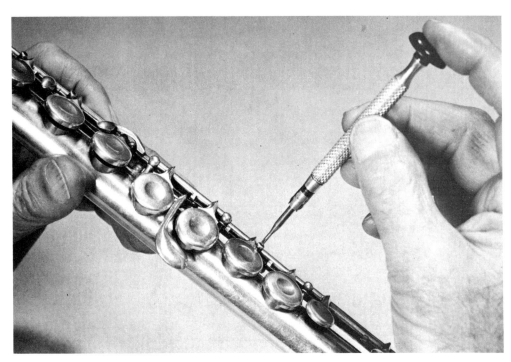

rectly. If the top pad is closing and the other pad is open, turn the screw to the left and it will raise the top key, permitting the other key to close. Use the same method to align the keys on the bottom stack.

7. Check the first finger B♭. If it does not produce B♭, the bridge key is usually at fault. The cork on the bottom of the upper key lap might be missing or the bridge keys could be bent. If the flute has adjustment screws on the bridge key, the screw probably needs to enter the key to a greater extent. Straighten bridge keys in the same manner described in Chapter 4, "Clarinet."

8. Hold down the pad cup that closes by the action of the bridge key—to produce B♭. Now, try moving the bridge key. If you feel any movement, the little wedge pin (small steel pin extending through the stack rod) needs further insertion to wedge the key on the rod more securely.

9. If the low C key is sticking, check the screw in the roller. This screw often works loose and backs out to where it catches on either the E♭ or C♯ key. In this condition, it can also hold the E♭ key open, making it impossible to play D, C♯ or C.

10. If B♭ will not play using first finger and thumb key #1, check for the following:

a. Cork may be missing from under the extension of the B♭ key that contacts the bottom end of the thumb key (key #1).

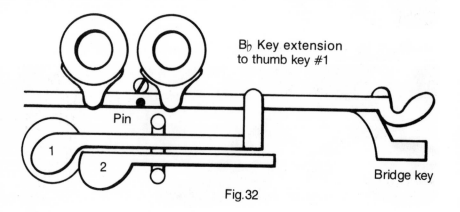

B♭ Key extension to thumb key #1

Pin

1

2

Bridge key

Fig. 32

b. Extension may be bent up.
c. Key #1 may be bent up to the point where it will not close the pad in key #2.

   d. Cork or felt under key #1 may be missing.

   e. Key #1 at thumb-tip end may be bent down to the point where it cannot raise the B♭ key extension.

11. Check for pad trouble (leaks). Using a leaklight, examine each pad. Look at the complete tonehole imprint on the pad. Is the pad skin broken or tonehole rim cut? Sometimes the rim cut is so thin or soiled that it is hard to detect. A large needle spring or small screwdriver tip might have to be used to lift the skin at the imprint to find the cut. If the pad is cut or broken it must be replaced, since it permits leakage.

12. Use the leaklight to check the trill key pads. The posts that hold these keys are located where they can easily be hit and bent. When bent to the point where they cause too much play, the key will move back and forth between posts, preventing the pads from seating properly. The posts may also become bent in the opposite direction, and bending the top post will pull or push the pads off their toneholes; if bent towards the toneholes, it will raise the pads in back, and if bent away from the toneholes, it will raise the pads in front.

Photo 29

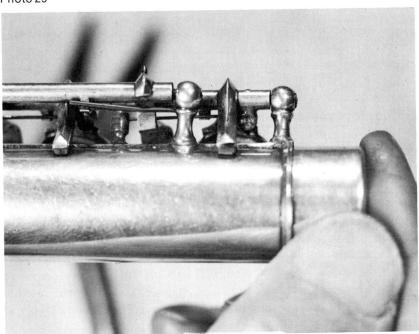

A bent bottom post will cause the pedal to ride on the spring of the D key and hold the pad open (*see photo 29*).

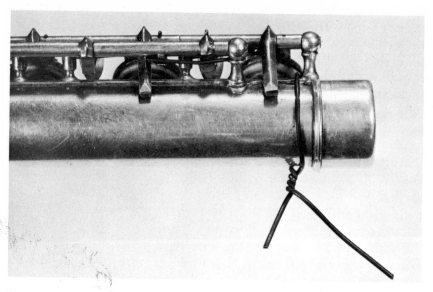

Photo 30

To correct: Look at the post to find which way it is bent; then with smallnose pliers bend it back perpendicular to the flute body. In some instances, the post is mounted on a rib which is soldered to the flute body. To keep from breaking the rib loose, bind it to the body of the flute by wrapping soft iron wire completely around it; then twist the wire with pliers until it is tight. Now, straighten the post (*see photo 30*).

13. If the mouthpipe (head joint) is difficult to insert in the flute, the bottom stack rod and keys are probably bent down. This may result from gripping the center of the bottom stack too tightly when pushing the two joints together. Check the bottom stack keys for leakage; if the pads are touching in back and light is emitting in front, this usually indicates that the bottom stack rod is bent. Hold the flute in a horizontal position at eye level and check the stack rod to see if it is swaybacked (curves downward in center). Now hold the flute lower and look straight down on the bottom stack. The rod is seldom bent straight down, but rather down and out toward the pad cups.

To correct: This condition can often be corrected by placing both first fingers at the ends of the stack (at post); close the keys and place your right thumb on the front of the F key and your left thumb on the front (outside pad cup) on the next key (middle finger F♯). Now apply *just enough* force to raise and straighten the stack rod.

14. Check the tuning slide cork in the mouthpiece (head joint). It should fit snugly. If it is loose, unscrew the crown until it is free; then push the cork through the large end of the mouthpiece. Note that the cork is threaded on the rod and there is a metal disc that holds the cork secure (*see photo 31*). Occasionally, however, you

Photo 31

will find the disc unscrewed and away from the cork. Tighten the disc so that it is firmly against the cork. The disc on the other end of the rod is permanently attached to the rod. After tightening the movable disc, rotate the rod as you wave the greased cork through the flame of a Bunsen burner. This will cause the cork to swell. Place the cork back in the mouthpiece, "screw-rod" towards small end; then with the flute cleaning rod push the cork in until the ring on the end of the rod centers in the tonehole. Replace the crown.

15. The keys of most flutes are made of German silver and will

not rust, but the rods are made of steel and may rust. The performer's right-hand fingers extend over the keys of the bottom stack and often touch the part containing the rod. Perspiration containing body acids and salt will work through the openings between the keys and onto the steel rods, causing them to rust. When this occurs, the keys will bind. If the keys do bind, *do not* stretch the springs to try to make the keys work easier.

To correct: Apply penetrating oil to the stack where the keys join, and work the keys up and down (as when playing) until free. You should see the oil work rust through the openings. After the key is free, apply key oil to the joint. If the key is frozen and will not budge, you will have to remove the wedge pins, disassemble the keys, and scour with steel wool to remove the rust.

16. If the mouthpipe (head joint) becomes bent or the foot joint keeps falling off, take the flute to your repairman. He has a tool for straightening and repairing these parts correctly.

17. If a flute is cleaned with silver polish, always oil the keys immediately afterward. Also be sure all polish is removed from the pads and springs. Note: This method of cleaning flutes is not recommended, but it is done occasionally.

18. If a wedge pin is missing from a stack rod, it may be replaced by a size .032 needle spring. Align the key with the pin hole and insert the spring tip until it binds. Clip the spring about $^1/_{16}$ inch above the rod, but do not cut the spring (wedge pin) too short or you will not be able to remove it easily when necessary. If the tip of the spring extends out too far at the bottom of the key, it must be clipped. Be sure the wedge pin is secure and there is no movement of the key on the rod.

19. If an annoying click appears when playing A it is probably caused by a bent B♭ auxiliary key; it is most likely bent down and hitting the top pad cup of the bottom stack (*see photo 32*).

Photo 32

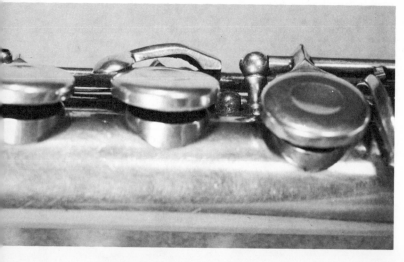

FLUTE PADS

The three small pads on the flute are the only pads installed with an adhesive and they are usually "floated in." The other pads have spuds (little tapered discs with a threaded hole in the center) which receive a screw and a small metal washer to hold the pad in place. Since this screw and washer hold the pad securely, there is no way for the pad to move to conform to the tonehole. It is impossible to seat a flute pad in the same manner as a clarinet pad.

The principal difficulty with most flute pad installations is encountered when forcing a pad that is too large to seat on the tonehole. The deeper the tonehole imprint on the pad, the greater the difficulty. Not only will the pad felt resist the tonehole, but the tone quality will be affected. Flute pads should be firm and absolutely flat when contacting the tonehole, and the imprint should be just deep enough to determine if the pad is seating correctly. These conditions will help insure a resonant, solid tone.

Pad Installation: Flute keys must be removed to install pads. Using a screwdriver with a broad edge, remove the screw and metal washer; then remove the old pad. There will probably be whole or parts of paper washers in the pad cup. Note if one is stuck to the old pad. There may also be a large metal washer present.

If paper washers were used, note where they were situated. There will probably be a discoloration either on the bottom of the old pad or in the bottom of the pad cup. If the new pad is the same thickness and the portions of paper washers are replaced in their original locations, the pad should seat perfectly. If there was a large metal disc, be sure to replace it. Place the pad in the cup and lay the key (pad down) on a flat surface, pressing firmly. This will distribute the pad evenly in the cup. Turn the key over; put the screw through the hole in the small metal disc, place it in the center of the pad and tighten the screw. Hold the edge of the pad so it will not turn when you tighten the screw. After installing the pad it will probably be wrinkled (*see photo 33*); to remedy, a pad iron must be used:

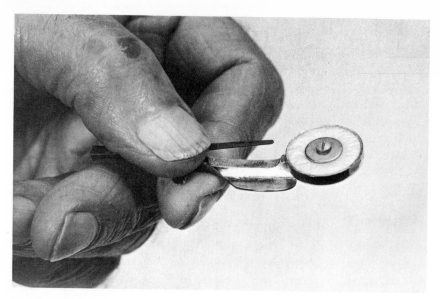

Photo 33

Dip the small end of the pad iron in water and slightly moisten the pad. If you get a surplus of water on the pad, simply wipe it off with a rag. Hold the small end or ring of the iron in a flame for a second or so, until warm (not hot or it will scorch the pad). It is a good idea to test the iron on a rag first; if it turns the rag

Photo 34

brown it is too hot. Place the ring of iron over the pad proper, encircling the metal pad washer (*see photo 34*). The wrinkles will disappear (*see photo 35*).

Photo 35

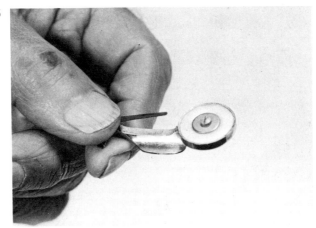

Replace the key instantly and hold it firmly against the tonehole for a few seconds. Check the pad seating with a leaklight under the pad to see if any bright light is emitting from anywhere around the pad. If it is, remove the key and look at the tonehole imprint on the pad. If there is no imprint on one side, or a very light imprint on one side and a deep imprint on the opposite side, remove the the pad and place a thin piece of paper washer in the cup where the imprint is shallow. Replace the pad and repeat the above procedure.

It might be necessary to repeat this operation several times until the pad seats satisfactorily. This is one reason why repadding a flute is difficult; each pad must seat perfectly with a light imprinting on the entire circumference of the pad.

Replacing a Spud: When the pad is removed, you might find the spud unsoldered, or the spud might break loose when you tighten the screw. To replace a spud, apply a very small amount of soldering acid to the solder remaining in the cup; hold the pad cup in a flame and place the spud in the center of the pad cup. When the solder becomes soft, remove the key from the flame, holding the spud in place until the solder cools or sets.

Replacing Small Pads: To replace the small flute pad, first remove the old pad with a pointed object. Since the pads have been floated in, do not heat the cup or disturb the cement. Put some shellac on the back of a new pad (usually size 11½) and press firmly to seat. If the cement adhered to the pad when it was removed, take the key off, remove the cement from the old pad and put it back in the cup. Then hold the cup at an even keel over the flame so the cement will cover the bottom of the cup evenly. Remove the cup from the flame and allow it to cool. Insert a drop of shellac in the cup and replace the pad.

If both the pad and cement are missing, you will need additional cement. It is available in two stick forms: one which you hold in a flame to melt and drip into the cup, and one with a wick that you light to melt the cement. Only two or three drops are needed to secure a pad. Hold the cup in the flame so the cement will spread evenly over the entire bottom of the cup. The pad can be applied to the cement while still tacky, but it is better to have the cement set first and then use shellac.

If the pad does not seat satisfactorily after replacing the key, heat the pad cup to soften the cement, then press lightly on the cup. The pad will pivot in the soft cement and conform to the tonehole. When using heat, always prick the edge of the pad with a pin to allow expanding air to escape. Do not overheat the pad cup or the cement will become too soft and be forced out from under the pad when the pad is pressed.

Sizes: Following are the pad sizes most frequently used for re-padding flutes:
    11, 11½, and 12 in the small size without holes.
    17½, 18, 18½ and 19 large size with holes.
Double-skin pads are highly recommended.

Caution: never use a pad that is too large even though it can be forced into the pad cup. This type of pad will bulge and never seat.

Flute pads can be obtained in several thicknesses and it is recommended, when ordering flute pads, that you state the make of flute(s) the pads are intended for.

You will also need paper washers in several sizes (17½, 18, 18½, 19) and in several thicknesses.

FLUTE QUICK-CHECK ROUTINE

1. Check if the rod on the first key (C) has backed out.
2. Check if any springs are unhooked.
3. Check the G♯ key pedal and pad.
4. Check the bridge keys.
5. Check the wedge pins.
6. Check the posts (top and bottom) C♯-D♯, C-D trill keys.
7. Check if all keys are moving on the rod.
8. Use a leaklight to see if any action is out of adjustment.
9. Look for defective pads.
10. Check the foot E♭ key.

SAXOPHONE

GENERAL CARE

■ Saliva should be drained from the instrument regularly. Difficulty in playing low C, B and B♭ may be due to a defective E♭ pad, which often results when students do not drain saliva from the saxophone. Consequently, when the instrument is placed in its case, the saliva drains down to the bottom E♭ key, which is held shut by spring action. Since this moisture cannot escape, it either settles on the E♭ pad and hardens the pad to the point where it can no longer seal, or rots the pad until it leaks. The top three left-hand palm keys (high D, E♭ and F) are also vulnerable to excess saliva.

■ Oil all moving parts periodically. Use a fine-grade oil and a small brush (or hypodermic-type oiler). Keep springs well oiled to prevent deterioration from rust. A large number of sax malfunctions are traced to the numerous moving parts.

■ Always place the end plug in the mouthpipe receiver before placing the saxophone in its case. This will prevent accidental bending of the octave key extension.

■ Bandbooks, folders, and other miscellaneous items should never be carried in the instrument case, unless a separate compartment is provided to prevent bent keys.

■ Promptly repair a defective kit catch in the sax case. Accessory boxes in saxophone cases are usually located near the bell of the sax and a defective kit catch will allow items to escape and enter the bell. Foreign items can get lodged in the body of the saxophone very easily.

■ Some baritone saxophone cases do not have a cushion or

case-fitting to cushion the center of the instrument, thus leaving the sax suspended from the low E♭ key guard to the bow or mouth-pipe receiver. When the weight of the instrument is concentrated in the center of the saxophone, a slight jar—caused, possibly, by setting the case down too hard—may bend the body and keys on the top stack. To prevent this from occurring, place a towel or cushion between the bottom of the case and the saxophone, approximately where the strap ring is located, to lessen the jolt.

PROBLEMS AND REPAIR PROCEDURES

Saxophones—with their numerous moving parts, soft keys, extensive use of cork to insure noiseless action, and vulnerable shape (especially true of the baritone sax)—require their fair share of classroom repairs.

Parts of the saxophone most susceptible to malfunction are:

1. Octave key mechanism
2. G♯
3. Side B♭
4. Low E♭
5. High D-E-E♭
6. F keys
7. Pads
8. Body

Octave Key Difficulties: This mechanism causes the most difficulty. Possible sources of trouble:

1. End plug not installed when placing sax in its case.
2. Mouthpiece and tenon receiver not maintained in clean and polished condition. A tight neck can be bent accidentally when forcing it into the sax tenon receiver or when removing it.
3. Pushing down on neck when forcing the mouthpiece on an ungreased cork.
4. Neck gripped too tightly when placing it in the sax, thus bending the neck octave key.
5. Neck not protected while it is in the case. Students often place the neck in the accessory box—which is generally filled with all kinds of odds and ends—and then force the lid closed.

6. Body extension rod not guided under the ring or foot of the neck octave key when entering the neck in the receiver.

The octave key mechanism on the saxophone has two ports or openings—one on the neck that opens for A and above, and one on the body that opens for G and below. One must close when the other opens. The octave key section on the neck usually causes the most trouble.

When you press the thumb key, only the octave key on the neck should open, and when you remove your thumb it should close *completely*.

When playing high A the neck key should open, and when going to G the key on the body should open and the one on the neck should close completely. When the procedure is reversed (going from G to A) the key action will be just the opposite.

When the octave key is not being used or when G is fingered with the octave key, there should be a tiny space between the extension of the body octave key mechanism and the ring or foot of the neck key which it contacts. This is the first place to check if the instrument is not functioning properly.

If there is no space between these parts, the neck octave key is probably not closing completely, thus hindering the lower register (*see photo 36*).

Photo 36

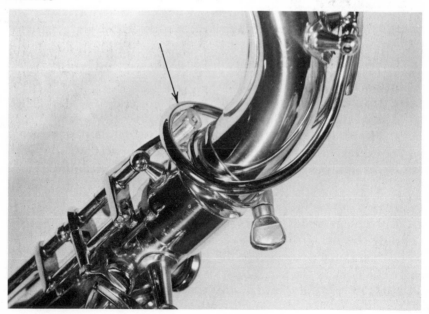

Three reasons why the neck octave key will not close:

1. The body extension that contacts the neck octave key is bent up (*see photo 37*).

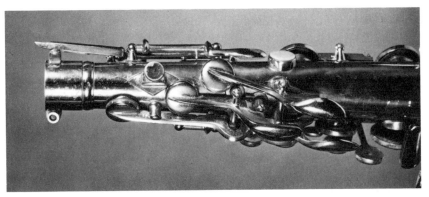

Photo 37

To correct: Using flatnose pliers, bend the extension down so it is parallel to the sax body.

2. The neck of the saxophone is bent down. This is easy to determine, since the tubing of the neck should be round. If the sides bulge or the tubing is oval, the neck is bent down. If the sides have a flat appearance, the neck has been bent up.

Photo 38

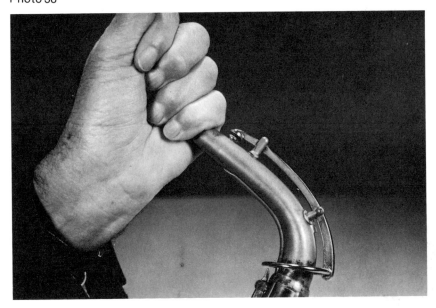

To correct: Place the neck in the body of the sax (playing position) and, if the neck is bent down, *gently* lift it up until the side bulges disappear (*see photo 38*). If the neck is bent up, reverse the procedure.

3. The neck octave key is bent.

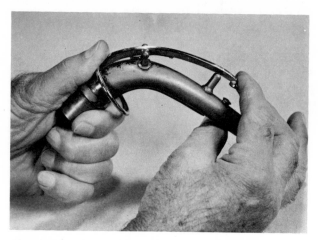

Photo 39

To correct: Hold the ring firmly against the neck and press down on the pad cup. Press the thumb octave key to see if the neck octave key opens. If it does not, the key was bent too much. Thus, reverse the bending procedure by holding the pad cup firmly and pressing up on the ring (*see photo 39*).

After obtaining the right bend so the neck octave key opens and closes correctly, try playing G (with the octave key) and see if the neck octave key closes completely. If it does not, the extension might require further bending.

The rod that extends from the top of the G key to the octave key mechanism may be bent and thus will not lift the bottom part of the extension key high enough to force down the end that activates the neck octave key ring. This might sound a bit confusing, but the extension that contacts the neck ring is on the opposite side of the rod and works like a lever—lifting one end lowers the other. It is more likely that the bottom part of the body extension key is bent up. Be careful not to bend this key down too much or the G key will not close. The top part of the body octave extension will hit the sax body.

One key to check at all times if you are having octave key trouble is the G key. It may be bent up. Check to see that the distance between the pad and the tonehole is the same as that on the top stack (C, B and A). If the G key is higher, hold the G pad cup, bend down the top part of the key (that contacts the octave key mechanism) with your flatnose pliers until the G key height is the same as the others.

When the saxophone cannot be played in the lower register, first check to see that there is a space between the octave key (neck) and the extension of the sax body that contacts it—when the octave key is not being used and when playing G with the octave key.

When the neck is straight and the keys appear to be in their proper position, but the octave key will not open, check the following: (1) the spring on the extension key may be unhooked; (2) the spring on the neck octave key (flat-type) is stronger than the one on the body extension. (3) The guide post that keeps the octave key in line could be bent and binding.

To correct: Either weaken the neck octave key spring by reducing its curve or strengthen the extension key spring. (See Chapter 3, "Springs," on how to strengthen needle springs.) Open the spread of the guide post to permit free movement of the octave key.

G♯ Key: Possible sources of trouble:

1. Two spring actions are working against each other, by low C♯, B, and B♭.

2. The G♯ key is bent.

3. The extension from the key above the F key is losing its cork or felt or is bent.

The G♯ pedal (the key pushed down with the little finger to play G♯) has a strong spring, which must be strong enough to overpower the spring on the pad key to close it completely. For this reason, the spring on the pad key is not as strong. However, it must be strong enough to open the pad key when the pedal key tension is removed. This pad frequently collects moisture. If the moisture contains sugar from chewing gum or a soft drink, it will cause the pad to stick and the light spring is not strong enough to break the seal and raise the pad. Do not change the spring tensions until you have tried cleaning the pad, which should be done in the following way: place a layer of rag between the pad and tonehole; hold the key down firmly on the rag and draw the rag from under it. This will clean both the pad and the tonehole.

If the G♯ pad cup does not close completely when you lift

your finger from the pedal, apply some cork grease to the parts that connect to produce the action (the part that extends from the pedal key to the extension of the pad cup).

G♯ key trouble is not only confined to producing the G♯ tone, but is frequently the culprit when other tones cannot be played. Some saxophones have an extension on the G♯ pedal that extends under the table keys for low C♯, B and B♭, which enables the player to obtain G♯ by pressing any of these keys. If you are unable to play the low tones C♯, B and B♭, check to see if the G♯ pad key is opening when you use any of these low tone keys.

There is an arm on the top of the F pad cup that extends over the G♯ pad cup. This extension should hold the G♯ key closed when playing the low tones. If it does not hold the G♯ key closed, check to see if the cork or felt is missing from under the extension. If missing, it must be replaced. If the cork or felt is not missing, bend this extension down with pliers until it closes the G♯ key. Be very careful not to bend it too much or the pad on the key with the extension will not close.

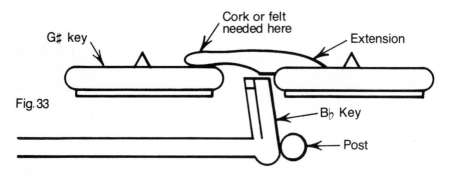

Fig. 33

The illustration above shows the first and second keys of the bottom stack, with the second key's extension over the first or G♯ key. It also shows the top stack B♭ key under the extension.

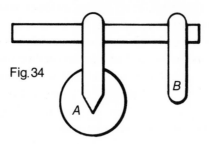

Fig. 34

Some saxophones have G♯ keys where extension C does not contact the G♯ pad cup A, but has an extension from its hinge tube B for contact. (*See Figs. 34 and 35.*)

Some G♯-bridge key mechanisms have adjustment screws at these points

Fig.35

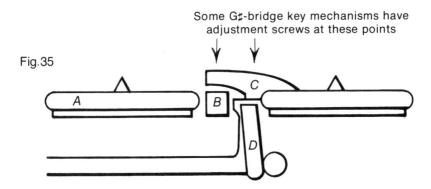

If G♯ key A does not close when depressing any of the bottom stack keys, hold G♯ key A and bend up on its extension B until the pad closes. If there are adjustment screws on the C extension to close either the G♯ key A or the B♭ key D (top stack), run these screws in further to eliminate space at contact points.

If you are unable to play G on saxophones with the G♯ key extension, check to see if the G♯ pad is closing. It might be held open by: (1) the table keys G♯, low C♯, B, or B♭ being bent; or (2) the bumpers on the low B or B♭ keys being too thick; or (3) the key guards over the low B and B♭ keys being bent in and pushing the keys down.

If the G♯ pedal is higher than the other table keys, check to see if the other table keys are down and holding the G♯ key pad open. If the G♯ key is bent up, return it to its proper level with pliers.

Side B♭ Key: When unable to play G or below, always check the side B♭ key. The side B♭ key pad cup is close to the strap ring and the hook from the neckstrap often catches under this key, either bending the key or tearing the pad.

High D, E♭, E and F Keys: High D, E♭, E, and F keys are close to the mouthpiece and are subjected to a great deal of moisture. They are also very easily bent off the toneholes; thus, when a saxophone does not play satisfactorily, always check these keys first with a leaklight. If these pads become hard as a result of excessive moisture, replace them. Hard pads will not seat.

Defective Pads, Bent Keys, Missing Corks: The only sure way to find leaking pads is with a leaklight. If you use the light, remove the neck and enter the light through the top of the saxophone. Proceed to the bottom, stopping behind each pad. Close the key to see if light is emitting from anywhere around the pad. If air is leaking from the side, this is a good indication that the pad is good but the key is bent.

To correct: Grip the extension (arm) that runs from the rod to the pad cup with your pliers and bend towards the side that leaks. If it is leaking in front, place a flat strip of metal between the back of the pad cup and the tonehole rim, then push down on the front of the pad cup. If it is leaking in back, you can correct the leak by removing the pad and placing a layer of adhesive (not cellulose) tape across the back of the pad. Use scissors to trim the tape to the shape of the pad; next apply shellac to the pad (including the tape) and replace it. If it still leaks, apply another layer. If you do not want to bend a key, you can use the adhesive tape method anywhere on the pad circumference when leak is visible. (For further details, see section on pad installation, and photos 43, 44, and 45.)

There are two rows of keys on the saxophone. The top row played with the left hand and the bottom row played with the right right hand. The rows are called stacks.

Just above the B key (first finger) you will see a small pad cup.

Photo 40

Press this pad cup down and you will see that it is attached to a long bar behind the stack, which rests on the feet of the C, B, and A keys (*see photo 40*). When playing any of these tones, not only must the pad under each of the keys you are pressing close, the small key at the top of the stack must also close. Between the feet of these keys and the bar is a piece of cork or felt which keeps the action silent. When this material is missing or worn, the pad in the small cup at the top of the stack will not close completely, and thus the saxophone will not function properly.

Check this pad with your leaklight under the small pad at the top of the stack and press the B key (first finger) to see if light is emitting from around the top pad. Repeat this procedure with the C key (second finger). If you detect light emitting in both instances, the pad in the small cup was probably watersoaked and shrunk. If so, replace the pad. If the pad is in good condition, the key with the bar extension may be bent.

To correct: Spread three fingers of your right hand and hold the bar firmly against the sax body. Press down on the small pad cup just enough to close the pad.

If the small pad closes when you press only one of the top keys (either B or C), but does not close when you press the other, this indicates that the cork or felt on the foot connection of the key that does not close it is either missing or too thin.

To correct: Place a thin piece of cork on the bottom of the bar where it comes in contact with the foot. Do not use cork which is too thick or the key you are pressing will not close.

Top Stack: There are five pad cups on the top stack and the 3rd and 4th cups must close in unison to produce the tone C (second finger). An extension containing the pearl button from the 4th cup rests on the 3rd cup, and beneath the pearl button is a felt disc. If this felt disc is missing, the 3rd cup will not close. If the 3rd and 4th keys do not close in unison, the extension (pearl key) will have to be bent. If the 3rd cup does not close, hold the 4th cup and bend the extension key down. If the 4th cup does not close, bend the extension key up.

The G key or 5th pad cup operates independently.

Bottom Stack: The bottom stack consists of five pad cups (*see photo 41*). The G$\sharp$, or top, cup may be mounted separately with its own posts and rod, or all five may be on one rod. This depends on the make or model of saxophone, although the action operates in the same manner.

Photo 41

The second cup has an extension over the G♯ key (1st cup) and is similar to the small pad cup above the top stack; that is, it has a long bar which rests on the feet of the three bottom keys (F, F♯, and D). When closing either the F, F♯, or D keys, the second cup with the extension over the G♯ key must also close. The bottom stack is aligned by the same method described for the top stack.

Low E♭ Key: Inability to produce low tones of the saxophone may be attributed to a faulty E♭ key. When students neglect to remove saliva by tilting the sax forward after playing, the saliva drains down onto the E♭ pad, with no way of escaping once the sax is placed in its case. Consequently, the pad hardens and can no longer seat, thus causing leakage.

Although the E♭ key has a guard over it, its location makes it vulnerable to harsh bumps—especially on the baritone saxophone. This guard is frequently bent down into the body, pulling the tonehole uneven; or the post at the end becomes bent, changing the angle of the pad-cup movement.

The pad in the E♭ key should be checked frequently and if it hardens it should be replaced. If it does not seat perfectly, the low tones will be difficult to produce and will most likely be distorted.

Since the low E♭ and C keys are usually on the same rod, bending the post will probably disturb the seating of the C key. But if the post does become bent, it can be straightened to its original position without disturbing the solder which seals the post to the body. The body material is quite soft, especially on newer model saxophones.

Straightening Toneholes and Pushing Out Dents: Serious dents can occur where key guards have been pushed into the body. Such repairs should be left to your repairman—he has the necessary tools for these operations.

C♯ Pad Not Seated: The low C♯ key post is also in a location where it can easily be hit and bent, which usually is the reason the C♯ pad does not seat. Another reason: the part on the table keys which is pressed to open the C♯ key is bent to a point where it binds on the low B table key.

Cannot Play Low B♭: Both the B♭ and B keys must close in unison. Since this key system is not the same on all makes of saxophones, it would be difficult to describe their functions, faults, and corrections without a great deal of confusion. However, check the table keys. There is a layer of cork or felt between the B♭ pedal and the B pedal and if it is missing the B key will not close when pressing the B♭ pedal. These pedals are frequently bent; consequently, if the B♭ pedal is bent down or the B pedal is bent up, the B♭ pad will not close. If the B♭ pedal is bent up or the B pedal is bent down, the B pad will not close.

To correct: Straighten the pedals so they are in line with each other and place the correct thickness of cork or felt between them so both pads will close when the B♭ pedal is pressed.

Binding Keys on Top Stack: If the top stack keys will not come up when the fingers are removed, this may very well be caused by a bent body. Remove the neck and sight down the sax body. If the body is bent, you will notice a curve in the rods, especially the long E natural key rod. *Do not* attempt to "unbend" a saxophone body—take it to your repairman.

Unable to Tighten Neck: Inability to tighten the saxophone neck is a frequent fault. If this occurs, first check to see if the tension screw is in correctly. Only one side of the ligature has threads, but the tension screw will enter the ligature from either side. The tension screw has a collar which presses against the side without threads and pulls the slot opening closed. If the screw is in correctly, but the neck still will not tighten, follow this procedure:

To correct: Using a small file (magneto type), file between the parts that the screw goes through to remove enough metal so that the neck will tighten (*see photo 42*).

Photo 42

Difficulty in Playing a Solid D (six fingers down): This is not always caused by a leak. It could be caused by the low C key being too close to the tonehole. Either the bumper felt is too thick or the key guard is bent down.

To correct: Slice off a piece of the felt bumper. If it is the adjustable type, back it out *one turn*. If the key guard is bent, straighten it to raise it off the key.

Lodged Hinge, Rod, or Pivot Screw: There is no simple way to remove a lodged hinge screw. If one becomes stuck, dab it with penetrating oil and allow it to set for thirty minutes. (It might help to heat the hinge or post, but you will then have to reapply the oil several times.) Always try to move the screw forward before attempting to back it out. If considerable difficulty is encountered, take it to your repairman and he will saw it out and replace it.

SAXOPHONE PADS

There are many varieties of saxophone pads and certain types of saxophones require installation of the original pad type.

Sizes: Some saxophone pads are sized in millimeters. Most, however, are in 32nds of an inch. Thus, a pad size 32 is $^{32}/_{32}$nds or 1 inch in diameter; a size 25 pad has a diameter of $^{25}/_{32}$nds.

A sax pad with ¹/₈-inch felt is usually adequate, although some saxophones require a little thicker pad.

Adhesive: Shellac is a good adhesive for securing pads, since it is insoluble in water and unaffected by excessive saliva and can be easily adjusted or removed by heating the pad cup.

Pad Installation: To find the correct size pad, measure the inside diameter of the pad cup. If the pad does not close or seat in front after insertion, it is too thick. If it will not close or seat in back, the pad is too thin.

After selecting the right pad, check to see that all of the old pad and adhesive have been removed from the pad cup. Place the new pad in the key cup and close the key. Press firmly enough to initiate a tonehole imprint on the pad. Raise the key and remove the pad and check the imprint. Can you see a complete circle? If a complete, even circle was formed, apply shellac to the back of the pad and return it to the key. Place a bottle cork or wad of paper between the key and guard (or between the key and bell if on the bottom stack) to hold the pad firmly against the tonehole until it seats. If replacing a pad on the top stack or side keys, place a wedge between the foot of the key and the sax body.

If the imprint on the pad does not form a complete circle, the key or pad is not level (flat) with the tonehole. To overcome this fault, do the following:

1. Put a layer of adhesive (not cellulose) tape on the bottom of the pad beneath the vague or missing imprint (*see photo 43*).

Photo 43

2. Using scissors, trim the excess tape to the shape of the pad (*see photos 44 and 45*).

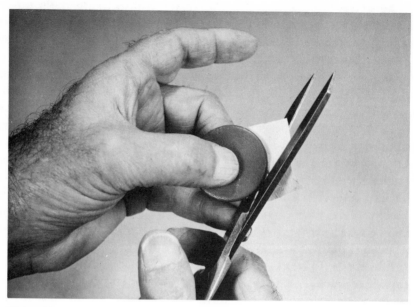

Photo 44

Photo 45

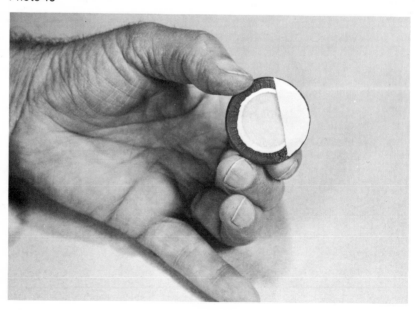

3. Apply shellac to the back of the pad (including tape) and install as described in previous paragraph.

After inserting the new pad, use a leaklight to check both the new pad and the pads in the keys that work in conjunction with the key just repadded. If other pads are badly worn or compressed from use or old age they, too, may have to be replaced.

Preserving Pads: When a saxophone is exposed to excessive saliva, a pad with the slightest leak will allow it to emerge. As the saliva travels through the inside of the sax it forms a path or channel (pattern) and will follow this path each time the sax is played, even though the defective pad has been replaced. That is why certain pads deteriorate rather frequently. To overcome this problem, push a cleaning brush or draw a rag through the sax body immediately after playing (while instrument is still moist). This will destroy the path or pattern the saliva has been following and permit it to flow on down to the bottom, where it will be allowed to run out of the bell by tipping the sax forward.

The inside of a sax should be cleaned regularly to save the pads and preserve the instrument's exterior finish. When a pad becomes saturated with saliva and is slapped down on the tonehole, the saliva spews onto the finish. If this saliva is not removed immediately, it will eat into the lacquer or plating after a few weeks. *Frequent swallowing will alleviate the excess saliva problem.*

Pads in Older Saxophones: Years ago, before woven felt was used in sax pads, the inside of a pad was very soft and thick. The cover (skiver) was drawn over this material and sewed in a drawstring manner, but did not have a glued back. It was necessary for the pads to be loose, since the rims of the toneholes were not level (even) and the pads had to give to conform to the tonehole's high and low spots.

Saxophones that use these particular pads are still found and it is impossible to use a new woven hard felt pad on such instruments—especially if they have tone reflectors on them. The only solution is to take the sax to your repairman and see if he can level the toneholes or use soft, thick pads by deep-seating them.

RECORKING

Recorking the Sax Neck: Take a sheet of $^1/_{16}$-inch cork and span the area covered by the old cork to determine the length of cork needed. Using a ruler and single-edge razor blade, cut a strip for the alto sax approximately $2^5/_{16}$ inches; for the tenor sax, approximately $2^1/_2$ inches; for the baritone sax, $2^3/_8$ inches. Bevel the edges for a lap of about $^5/_{16}$-inch. The bevel must be opposite on the ends, as illustrated:

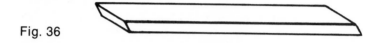

Fig. 36

When wrapped around the neck tube, the cork will look like this:

Fig. 37

If a cork is old or dry it will break when bent around the tube. To make the cork pliable, place it in a smooth-jaw vise and press. Do this before you cut the desired width and length, since pressing will expand the cork.

Cover the part of the neck to be corked and the bottom side of the cork with liquid shellac. (For fast adherence, contact cement may be preferred.) Hold the shellacked part of the neck over the flame, allowing the shellac to boil. Then, wrap the cork (shellacked part down) around the tube and hold in place momentarily until it sets. Wrap rubber bands around the cork (size 33 recommended) while holding the lap down all the way across the cork. Let it cool.

After the cork has cooled and the rubber bands have been removed, the cork is ready for use. It may be necessary to rag the cork with strips of sandpaper to obtain a perfect fit. However, if you want a finished job, wrap the cork with cloth tape and tie the ends. Reduce the flame on your torch to a fine tip and allow it to enter the end of the tube until the shellac oozes from the cork ends. Let it cool; then remove the tape. The cork will be smooth, but you might have to rag it with fine-grade sandpaper to obtain the correct size for the mouthpiece. Be sure to apply cork grease before placing the mouthpiece on the cork.

Procedure:

1. Cover the bottom side of the cork with liquid shellac (*see photo 46*).

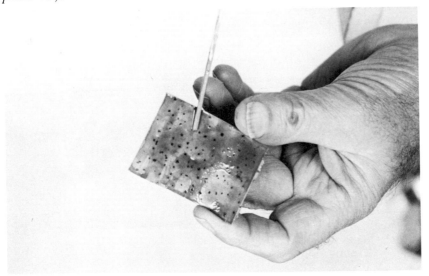

Photo 46

2. Cover the cork lap with liquid shellac (*see photo 47*).

Photo 47

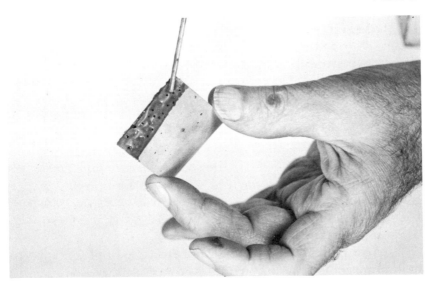

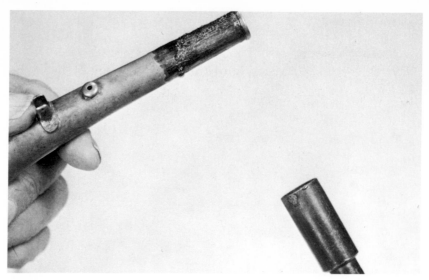

Photo 48

3. Hold the shellacked part of the neck over the flame, allowing the shellac to boil (*see photo 48*).

Photo 49

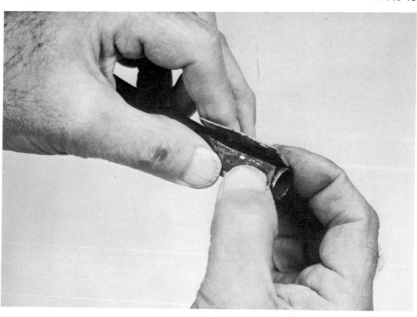

4. Wrap the cork (shellacked side down) around the tube and hold in place momentarily until it sets (*see photo 49*).

Photo 50

5. Wrap the cork with rubber bands (size 33 recommended) while holding the lap down all the way across the cork (*see photo 50*). Allow it to cool.

6. For a "finished" job, wrap the cork with cloth tape and tie the ends (*see photo 51*).

Photo 51

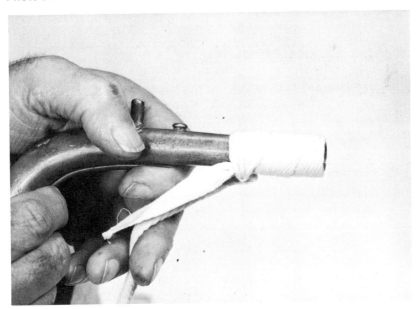

7. As the final step, reduce the flame on your torch to a fine tip and let the flame enter the end of the tube until the shellac oozes out the cork ends. Let the tube cool; then remove the tape.

Remedying Shrunken Neck Cork: If a saxophone neck cork seems to be in good condition, but has shrunk to the point where it is too small to hold the mouthpiece properly, apply cork grease to the cork and wave the cork through the flame of a Bunsen burner or torch. The heat will expand the cork. *Move the neck rapidly enough so the cork will not ignite.* Wipe off the cork grease and allow the cork to cool before replacing the mouthpiece.

Applying Cork Instantly to Keys:

1. Cut a piece of cork of the correct thickness to the approximate size needed to cover the key.

2. Cover the part of the key where cork is to be applied with liquid shellac.

3. Hold the key over a flame until the alcohol burns and the shellac bubbles.

4. Withdraw from the flame while still bubbling and place the cork on the shellac, holding firmly for a second or until it cools; it will adhere instantly.

5. Trim to exact key shape.

SAXOPHONE QUICK-CHECK ROUTINE

1. Is there any foreign item in the saxophone body? If the sax produces no sound at all—or just a few upper tones—remove the neck and look down into the body. You will probably find an end plug, mouthpiece cap, or even a can of cork grease lodged inside.
2. Are any pads missing?
3. Is a spring unhooked or broken?
4. Is the felt disc missing from under the C key finger button?
5. Is the octave key holding open?
6. Is the G♯ key holding open?
7. Is the cork or felt missing from between the feet of the top stack keys and the long bar that rests on their feet?

8. Is the side B♭ key bent away from the tonehole or the side C key bent so that it is touching the bar of the top stack keys?
9. Is cork or felt missing from the bridge key that extends over the G♯ key and B♭ extension?
10. Is saliva emerging at one of the pads?
11. Use a leaklight to check all pads for leaks.

OBOE

The oboe—and, especially, the full-system oboe with its complicated mechanisms—is a delicate instrument, which usually requires the attention of a professional repairman. However, you can check several strategic spots where some 75 per cent of all oboe trouble originates.

Since the oboe has many adjustment features, be sure to examine the instrument closely and isolate the particular malfunction before undertaking any corrective work. Above all, exercise extreme care, for it is possible to disturb the entire mechanism in the course of attempting a repair.

PROBLEMS AND REPAIR PROCEDURES

1. The top post on the right little finger C key turns and binds the key. The key extends at an odd angle and if it is pressed on the side rather than on the top, the force will turn the post. (If this malfunction causes continuous trouble, be sure to show the student how to contact the key.)

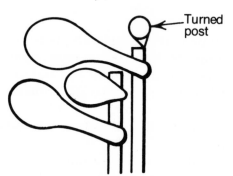

Fig.38

To correct: Straighten the post with pliers so the pivot screw enters the key properly. Always check the C key post first since it is most frequently turned. If the post is loose, unscrew it about two full turns; then apply pumice or the scrapings from fine sandpaper to the base of the post. Return the post to its original position; it should now be tight.

2. The second octave key spatula or pedal extends out to a point where it can easily be bent by a blow or a faulty case, and thus the bottom post is easily turned. If the post turns, the key will not function. Also, if the post is turned or the spatula bent, they will contact the leg of the C♯-D trill key and hold it open just enough to prevent the oboe from playing.

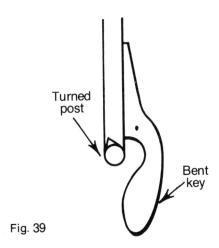

Turned post

Bent key

Fig. 39

To correct: Straighten the post with pliers to allow the screw to enter the key properly. If the post is loose, tighten it as described above (1). If the key is bent, hold the rod and straighten the pedal.

3. The left bridge key (in playing position) occasionally becomes bent or its bottom post turns. This is usually caused by carelessness when assembling the oboe. Like other keys, this key will not function properly when the post is turned. If the top bridge key is bent down or the bottom section bridge key is bent up, the C♯-D trill key will be held open.

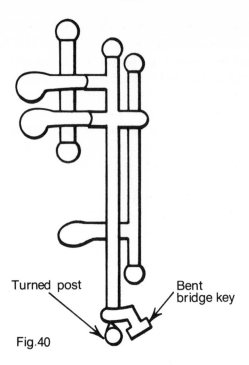

Turned post   Bent
                                           bridge key

Fig.40

To correct: Straighten the post, if turned; or tighten the post, if loose (as described in 1). Straighten the bridge keys with small flatnose pliers until they align with very little play between connecting parts. Always check the two small closed trill keys at the top of the oboe to see that they are not being held open due to the malfunction noted here.

4. The right bridge key (in playing position) becomes bent. Check the two small closed keys on the top stack, between the first and second and third fingers. Press each key with your finger. If you feel any movement, the keys are not closing properly. If both keys are not seating, the top bridge key is probably bent down or the bottom bridge key is bent up. Thus, the top bridge key cannot get low enough to activate the hinge of the key to force the two small keys on the top stack to close.

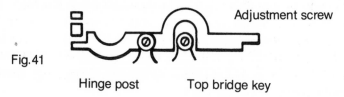

Adjustment screw

Fig.41

Hinge post   Top bridge key

To correct: Use flatnose pliers to straighten the bridge key that is causing the malfunction. If the bridge key is satisfactory but the two small keys are not closing, check the adjustment screw where the top end of the bridge key contacts the stack keys. Tighten this screw until the keys close.

If only one of the small keys does not close, the adjustment screw will eliminate the trouble. Do not turn the screw in too far or the second and third pads or corks will not close.

GENERAL MAINTENANCE

Maintaining Tenon Joint Corks: Caution oboe players to keep the tenon joint corks greased. Failure to do so usually results in bent keys or turned posts, as a result of forcing the joints together.

Pad Replacement: Replacement of an oboe pad requires expert ability and should normally be done only by a professional repairman. However, if a pad falls out and *emergency* replacement is required, follow this procedure:

Apply a small amount of shellac to the back of the pad and try to place it in its original position without disturbing the material in the pad cup. This should hold until the instrument can be taken to a repairman.

OBOE QUICK-CHECK ROUTINE

1. Check the high C♯-D trill keys to see if they are closing.
2. Check to see if any of the posts are turned.
3. Check the extension from the bottom stack to the G♯ key to see that it is not bent down to the point where the first key (F) on the bottom stack cannot close or raise the bridge key (right-hand side) that opens the two small pad keys on the upper stack to play C̄. There is also an adjusting screw in the end of this extension key that might be in too far.
4. Check bridge keys on left-hand side to see that they are not bent but parallel.
5. Check the screw from the bottom C key to the E♭ key to see that it is not in so far that it keeps the C key from closing completely.

6. Check the two octave key pads to see if they are opening, especially if they are of a synthetic material.

7. Check the extension on the left-hand low B key and the bell joint bridge keys to see that they are straight, so that both keys, B and B♭, will close when pressing down the B♭ key to play low B♭.

8. Check the spring of the low E♭ key to see that it rides completely in the center of the key on the end, as this spring also operates the B key. The C key extension also rides under this key. As this mechanism varies in structure on different models of oboes it is difficult to describe. Just remember, however, to get the spring in the center of the E♭ key at the end. (Some oboes have a groove for this spring to ride; others do not.)

CORNET AND TRUMPET

GENERAL CARE

- Rinse mouth before playing instrument.
- Always blow saliva out of instrument after playing.
- Clean the mouthpipe weekly with a flexible cleaner. If the mouthpipe is a curved one-piece unit, the best type of cleaning apparatus is a wool swab with bristles—it's firm and will clean more thoroughly than other types. (Be sure to use a cornet-trumpet cleaner, not a sax neck brush.) If the instrument has a curved mouthpipe, use the same kind of cleaning device.

Weekly cleaning of the mouthpipe is one of the most important items in the care of the cornet-trumpet—it will eliminate virtually all valve trouble and keep the instrument in peak playing condition. A catch-all, the mouthpipe is first to receive discharges from the mouth—air, saliva, food particles, acids, lime, sugar, and a host of other substances. All, except air and saliva, remain in the mouthpipe.

If the mouthpipe is not cleaned regularly, this foreign matter will accumulate and line the inside of the tubing, hindering the instrument's performance. When the cornet-trumpet is not in use, the accumulation of substances dries, forming a crust. When air is forced back into the instrument, loose particles from this crust are blown into the valve ports and work their way onto the valves.

Since there is no space between the valve and casing for the particles to escape, the valves do not function properly.

A damaging crust is also formed when a mouthpipe lined with foreign matter containing lime comes in contact with a particle of food containing acid. The chemical reaction produces a crust that continues to grow until it works its way through the metal. Little orange-pink spots which may appear on the mouthpipe tubing do not originate on the outside—they grow from the inside. A chemical crust under an orange-pink spot can be seen when you remove the main tuning slide and look through the mouthpipe. If you look closely at the outside spot with a magnifying glass, you might see a tiny hole in the very center. Your repairman can secure a small patch over the spot, but it is best to replace the entire mouthpipe since other spots are probably ready to emerge. Again —the best preventive: keep the mouthpipe clean to forestall damage.

■ Clean the valve ports by using a small brush or by drawing a soft piece of cloth through each port.

■ Oil the valves periodically.

■ Prevent sticking of slides through frequent lubrication. If a slide lubricant is not available, use cork grease or petroleum jelly.

■ Prevent rusting—and eventual breakage—of water key springs by regular oiling. A drop of oil can be placed on the springs when oiling the valves.

■ Keep the bottom valve caps clean. Dust and dirt particles that work their way into the cornet-trumpet frequently settle in the caps. With movement of the instrument—or even use, through the operation of bottom-type valve springs—this foreign matter can be dislodged and settle on the valves.

■ Caution players not to slap the mouthpiece with the cup of the hand when placing it in the instrument—lodging of the mouthpiece may result through such carelessness.

■ Bandbooks, folders, and miscellaneous items should never be carried in the instrument case unless a separate compartment is provided for such a purpose. This precaution will prevent bending of the middle valve slide.

■ Record each instrument's serial number. Instruments of the same make, model, and type are identical in appearance. However, there is a specific serial number to distinguish each instrument. The number is usually located on the valve casing and most instruments also have the serial number on the top of each valve (a fact that many people are not aware of). If an instrument is stolen or lost, the only positive way to claim ownership is by supplying the serial number. When several instruments of a specific kind are used in school, it is rather easy for students to exchange instruments unknowingly. Accordingly, it is good practice to list the instruments' serial numbers next to the students' names in your roll book. Most music stores keep a permanent list of all serial numbers of the instruments sold; therefore, if an instrument is stolen or lost and the student does not have the serial number, contact the dealer.

PROBLEMS AND REPAIR PROCEDURES

The cornet and trumpet are two of the sturdiest instruments in the band and, if properly cared for and maintained, should provide years of trouble-free service. However, they are also the most neglected instruments, which leads to some of the problems described here:

Hindered Tone Quality: If the tone quality seems to be hindered or constricted, hold the mouthpiece up to the light and look through it. As noted above, lime deposits from saliva tend to build up inside the stem of the mouthpiece, decreasing size of the opening and deadening the sound. Remove the accumulation with a mouthpiece brush.

Jammed Mouthpiece: If a mouthpiece puller is not available, lay the mouthpiece on firm wood and tap receiver with a rawhide mallet. Never use pliers, door jamb, or pipe wrench to dislodge a mouthpiece; you will mar and twist the mouthpipe and break the braces.

Difficult to Play: If the instrument is difficult to play, depress a valve about half the distance of its movement and try moving it sideways in the casing. If there is considerable movement, the valve is worn and leaking. If the valve fits firmly, remove it and examine each valve port. Corrosion can eat a hole through the port lining, making the instrument almost impossible to play.

Obstruction in Air Flow: Each valve casing is numbered on the outside (1, 2, 3) and the valves are numbered correspondingly on the top of the valve or on the valve stem. Each valve must enter its respective casing. If the instrument cannot be played at all, a valve is most likely in the wrong casing or turned to where the ports do not align.

Some instruments will respond (but to a very limited extent) when the 1st and 3rd valves are switched. Whenever a piston-valve instrument does not work properly, always check the valves first.

Bent Shank End of Mouthpiece: Use a center punch (tapered so that the small end enters the shank end of French horn mouthpieces and the large end fits bass mouthpiece shanks) as shown in photo 52.

Photo 52

Lodged Slides: If the slides are lubricated frequently, they will never become lodged. If they are lodged, your repairman is well equipped to dislodge them without damage to the instrument. In an emergency, however, try this procedure:

Photo 53

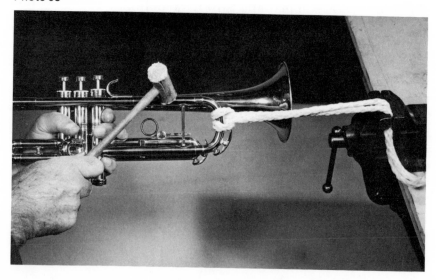

Using a soft rope, put a double loop around the slide bow. Attach the other end of the rope to a solid object (bench vise) and gently tap the tubing with a rawhide mallet, as you keep steady tension on the rope while holding the instrument at the valves (*see photo 53*). It might help to heat the tubing *lightly* by quickly drawing it through the flame of a Bunsen burner—a few times only. Certain lubricants become tacky. When heat is applied, it allows the slide to move.

Never attempt to pull slides while the valves are out of the instrument—you will spring the valve casings.

Never use hard or single strand rope to pull the main slide—you will dent the tubing.

Do not become too determined or reckless when pulling slides. If a slide does not move with the tension and tapping method without too much effort, *do not* use additional force or attempt any other method. Take it to your repairman.

Water Keys Not Closed Completely: Inspect the keys. Rust may cause the spring pressure to bind the screw and prevent the key from closing completely.

To correct: Loosen the screw about one-half turn and oil the spring.

Water Key Springs Broken or Defective: The water key rests in a saddle with a screw extending through the posts on each side, on which the key hinges. There are two types of water key springs: (1) the spring fits on the inside of the key; (2) the spring wraps around each side of the key hinge tubes.

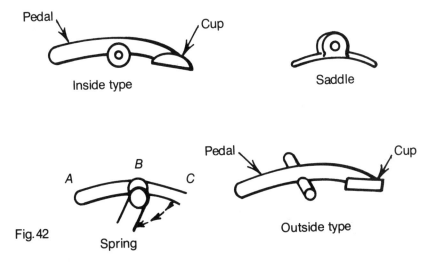

Fig. 42

To replace inside-type spring: Remove the key and the broken spring parts. Place a new spring (*B*) inside the key, with part (*A*) under the pedal and the tips (*C*) pressed back against the base of the saddle and pointing in the opposite direction of the water key nipple. Hold the spring firmly in the key and press the key down in the saddle so the coil (*B*) will line up with the screw holes on each side of the saddle. Insert the screw through the hole in the outside saddle post and on through the coil (*B*) into the inside saddle post. (The difficult part of this procedure is holding the spring—the spring tension fights back.) If a steel spring is installed clip the ends (*C*).

Caution: Hold the instrument away from your face when clipping the spring, or turn your head so the clipped parts cannot hit you. Also, do not clip springs in front of another person.

To replace outside-type spring: Place one coil (*B*) over one side of the hinge tube. Spread the spring; then slip the other coil over the remaining tube with the loop (*A*) under the pedal. Using pliers, press the loop (*A*) together so the coils fit snugly to the key. Push the key down in the saddle with the points (*C*) forced back under the pedal, resting on the saddle (pointing in the opposite direction of the water key nipple). Force the key down until the screw enters the saddle post and continues on through the hinge tube to the inside post.

If a *steel spring* is used, clip the ends as previously described.

If a *bronze or brass spring* is used, grasp end (*C*) with pliers and pull. This will tighten the coil on the hinge. Pull and bend the spring tips around the post (toward the water key nipple) and clip excessive wire.

Water Key Corks Defective: When installing new water key corks, note that they are slightly larger than the water key cups and must be forced to fit. To install a water key cork be sure, first, to remove all bits of the old cork. One side of the cork is usually smooth and free from holes and cracks, so apply a little shellac to the *opposite* side and force the cork in the cup. If it seems a little too large, use your thumbnail or small end of a pad slick to push the protruding part into the cup. Using the flat side of the slick, press the cork evenly into the cup. Hold the key closed firmly enough to see if it seats. You might have to use the slick to adjust the cork in the cup so that it is parallel to the nipple rim.

Lodged Valve Caps (top or bottom): Tap the caps with a rawhide mallet. This will break the seal and you will be able to turn them easily. Never use pliers or a pipe wrench to loosen lodged valve caps.

VALVES

In dealing with valves, it is essential to observe the following points:

Instruct students to remove only one valve at a time when they are being cleaned and oiled. This eliminates any possibility of placing a valve in the wrong casing.

Valves have a set movement (distance they should move). If this is correct, the valve ports and casing ports will align. To keep the valves noiseless, there is a cork or felt washer on each stem between the valve proper and the valve cap and also in the finger button (tip), or in the top of the valve cap.

All three valve stems should be the same height. If the cork or felt is missing, or if the felt has become oil-soaked and thus pressed flat between the valve and the valve cap, the valve will be too high. In most instances, there is a ring on the valve stem which will align with the top of the valve cap when the felt or cork is correct.

To determine if the felt or cork in the finger button is the correct thickness, remove the middle valve slide and depress the valve. The port (hole) in the valve and casing should coincide. Use the same method to check the felt in the top of the valve cap.

Of equal or greater importance than the correct felt thickness when the valve is depressed is the thickness of the cork and felt combination on top of the piston, which makes the ports align on the *up* stroke. This thickness must be accurately measured.

Valve guides—although of varying designs—have one common purpose: to keep the valve from turning. Piston valves must not turn while in the casing, since the ports of the valves must align with the casing knuckles to provide the valve with a guide. The most common type of valve guide is a small, oblong extension at the top of the valve which fits into and slides up and down in a slot in the valve casing. Other types have two or three extensions. These are called valve stars. If a valve guide has more than one extension, one of them will probably be wider than the other. Look down into the valve casing and note the slots. One of the slots will be wider; thus, when inserting the valve, turn it so that the wide extension will enter the wide slot and the valve will be in correctly. Since there are—as noted—many types of valve guides and spring actions, use complete caution to see that the valves are inserted properly.

VALVE PROBLEMS AND REPAIR PROCEDURES

Valve Will Not Go Down Completely: If the valve will not go all the way down when depressed, the valve spring is probably too long. If it is a bottom-type valve spring, the bottom ring of the spring (largest coil)—which fits into an indentation in the bottom of the cap—has slipped out.

To correct: If the spring is too long, replace it with a shorter spring. If the bottom-type valve spring has slipped out, remove the cap and rotate the spring until it works back into the groove.

Middle Valve Sticks: One of the most common reasons for impaired valve action is the presence of music sheets, school books, and other miscellaneous items in the instrument case, which require the case to be forced shut. This puts pressure on the middle valve slide and springs the casing. If the middle (2nd) valve sticks, push up on the slide with the base of your palm (*see photo 54*). If this is the cause of the problem, the valve will jump up when pressure is applied.

Photo 54

Dent in Casing: This may result from carrying the mouthpiece loosely in the case. If the valve moves only a limited distance and then stops, check the outside valve casing for a dent. If you find a dent, remove the valve, hold the instrument up to the light, and look through the casing. You will find a bump just the size of the outside dent—but inverted.

To correct: If it is impossible to take the instrument to a repair shop or if you need it immediately, remove the bump from the inside casing with a scraper. Be careful to scrape only the bump and not the entire casing. (Your repairman will probably use a steel mandrel just the diameter of the valve to push the dent out—without harming the surface of the casing. It is suggested, therefore, that you take the instrument to him.)

Sprung Valve Casing: To check if the casing is sprung, remove the piston from one of the other casings (one that works properly) and try it in the casing of the valve where trouble is occurring. If it also binds, this indicates a damaged casing.

Bent Piston: To check if the piston is bent, try it in one of the other casings. If it works freely, the piston is not defective. To check the piston and casing more closely, remove the bottom valve cap and see if the piston will enter and rotate freely. If the piston works freely in this process and in the exchanging process, the trouble is either with the valve guide or the stem. If either the casing or piston is sprung, take the instrument to your repairman, who has the tools to correct this malfunction.

Defective Valve Guide: Some valve guides are soldered onto the piston; others are screwed on. The screw type may work itself loose until it is no longer parallel with the piston and will bind in the slot in the casing. If the guide is not straight, use flatnose pliers to tighten and align the guide. Some guides are held in place by a locknut or screw and if a guide becomes loose it will not function properly.

Valve guides on older instruments may wear thin and the person inserting the valve may miss the slot, thus lodging the valve.

To correct: To free such a lodged valve, remove the valve cap and place one of the other valves in the casing—but from the bottom *(see photo 55)*. Remove the finger button and tap the end of the valve stem with your rawhide mallet. Never try to force a lodged valve out with a drumstick or anything smaller than the outside diameter of the valve. There is a metal cap in the bottom of the valve and if it is spread enough to cause binding, severe damage may result.

Photo 55

Bent Valve Stem: To check for a bent stem, remove the finger button and depress the valve to see if the stem binds against the side of the hole in the valve cap. If it does, raise the valve and tap the binding side of the stem with a rawhide mallet to straighten it.

CORNET AND TRUMPET QUICK-CHECK ROUTINE

1. Be certain that valves (pistons) are in their respective casings and that valve guides are in correct position.
2. Inspect for missing water key cork—or see if water key is holding open.
3. Look through mouthpiece while holding up to light.
4. Check for hole in mouthpipe or for unsoldered tubing.
5. Look for hole in piston ports.

CHAPTER

TROMBONE

GENERAL CARE

Although a trombone has only five movable parts—hand slide, tuning slide, bell-slide connection, mouthpiece, water key—this instrument frequently fails to provide maximum service. The reason: neglect. In virtually every band, inspection of trombones will turn up these defects (among others): hand-slide bow bent in; dents in tuning-slide bow; bent water key; defective water key cork; dirty inner slide or retarded slide action caused by sprung, dirty or dented slide.

These conditions are progressive—they occur and worsen over a period of time. Nevertheless, few trombones are repaired before the damage becomes extensive. Trombones are vulnerable to accidents because of their shape—but most damage is due to carelessness. Trombone students, new and old, should be given complete instructions on the care of their instrument, with emphasis on the following procedures:

■ Trombone players should be cautioned to set the instrument down on the hand-slide bow without excessive force. The bow has a protective guard with an extension for floor contact. However, the brass is soft and bends easily. Collapsing the bow will affect the tone and spring the slide.

■ Water keys should not be opened with the feet (a common practice among students). Such procedure may dent or spring the slide, or may bend the water key to a point where the cork no longer centers on the nipple.

■ When assembling the trombone, the slide should be kept at 180 degrees (straight)—the bell section directly opposite the mouthpiece. The slide should then be moved to a 90-degree angle (playing position) and the bell-lock screw tightened. If the trombone is assembled in the playing position, there is a good chance that the slide will loosen and hit the rim of the bell, thus denting the slide.

■ Be sure the slide takes its correct position in the case. Prevent the end that enters the bell section from contacting and possibly denting the bell.

■ Students should not slap the mouthpiece with cup of the hand when placing it in the instrument—this may lodge the mouthpiece.

■ Loose items in the carrying case can damage the instrument —brass is soft and dents easily. Students should carry mouthpiece and oil bottle in separate compartment.

SLIDE CARE

Cleaning Slides: Trombonists should clean the inside as well as the outside slide. If the inside slide is not cleaned regularly, small blisters will erupt on the plating. The blisters will eventually peel, requiring replacement of the inner slide.

Both a flexible and a rigid cleaning rod are recommended for cleaning the slides. The best flexible type has a wool and bristle swab. Be sure to obtain a *trombone* cleaning device, long enough to push through the bow. Insert the cleaner as far as you can, then withdraw it. Force water through the same side so it will expel the dirt that accumulates in the bow through the opposite end of the slide.

The rigid cleaning rod has an eyelet to insert a rag. Do not use a short strip of rag; use one long enough to provide a protruding tab. When the rod is turned and the rag wrapped around it to form a swab, part of the rag should not enter the tubing. This will allow you to pull out the swab if it becomes lodged. *Do not fail* to loop the rag over the eyelet in the rod to prevent ridges in the tubing (slide). If the rag does become lodged in the tubing, twist the rod and push it forward in the tubing to make the rag smaller. Continue to twist the rod as you withdraw it. In the event a student does use a short piece of rag which comes off the rod and lodges in the tubing, do

not try to burn it out. Take it to a gas station and blow it out with
an air gun.

Exercise extreme caution when cleaning the inner slide. The
upper section (which receives the mouthpiece) has a mouthpipe

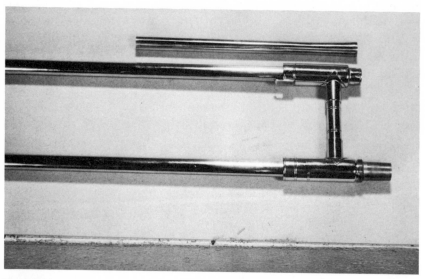

Photo 56

that enters the slide to about eight inches (*see photo 56*). To clean
this slide, use the flexible-type cleaner (bristle and wool). Never
force a rigid cleaning rod through the top inner slide.

If cold cream is used on a slide, the bow must be cleaned
frequently. Use a flexible cleaner and insert until it passes through
the entire bow or crook. Then, using water or an air hose in the
same side of the slide that the cleaner was inserted, force the
accumulation through the other side.

Oiling Slides: Students should be advised to keep trombone slides
oiled. Saliva, containing mouth acids and sugar, coats the slide and
impairs the action. Applying oil to a slide in this condition will not
correct the problem since the coating is not oil-soluble. The slide
must first be cleaned with soap and water. Fill the slide with a
soap and water solution and work the slide up and down. Rinse
in the same manner with clear water. Dry the outside of the inner
slide with a rag and the inside of the outer slide with a rod and rag.
Now, apply oil to the slides and instruct the student to keep them
oiled.

Draining Slides: Trombonists should be instructed to open the water key and release the saliva *each time* the instrument is used—before placing the slide in its case. Seventy-five per cent of all slide trouble is caused by failing to release the saliva. Trombones are frequently taken to repair shops to have the slide straightened or dents removed when the only trouble is actually a dirty slide. Placing the slide in its case without first draining it permits the saliva to run back on the slide, where it dries. Although you can see the deposit of this material only on the outside of the inner

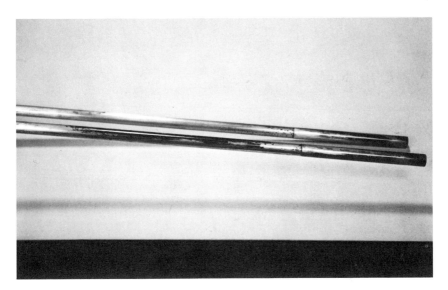

Photo 57

slide (*see photo* 57), the same accumulation gathers on the inside of the outer slide. Slide oil will not remove this material since it is not soluble by oil. If a trombonist has a lot of acid in his saliva this material cannot be wiped off; it must be buffed. If you find a slide in this condition and it cannot be wiped with a rag, take the trombone to your repairman, who will remove the accumulation before it eats into the plating. Then, instruct the student to drain his trombone after each use.

To check if students are draining their slides, look at the outside of the bell flare. If water spots are present, this indicates that the student is not draining the slide. Consequently, when the case is set up on end, the saliva runs back out the slides and down the bell.

PROBLEMS AND REPAIR PROCEDURES

Click in the Slide: If there is a metallic click when moving to first position or if the slide will not stay locked because it is too loose, the bumper cork or felt is most likely missing.

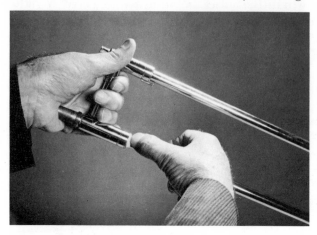

Photo 58

To correct: Cork or felt rings, available commercially, can be slipped over the end of the slide and forced into position by pushing the outer slide all the way in; or a piece of $\frac{1}{8}$-inch cork or felt about $1\frac{9}{16}$-inch long and $\frac{3}{16}$-inch wide may be used. Wrap the material around the inner slide and force it in with your thumbnail (*see photo 58*). Then use the outer slide, as shown in the illustration (*see photo 59*).

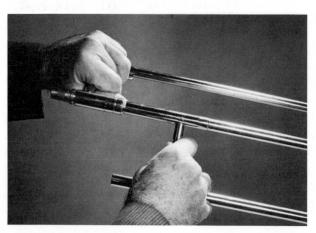

Photo 59

Tuning Slide Lodged: The tuning slide should be lubricated frequently, but never remove the slide by grasping the tubing or bow. One side of the tubing is larger than the other and the large side will receive the most force because it fills more of the hand. As a result, the larger side will emerge first, with the small side possibly bent. Both hands should be used when removing the tuning slide, either by bracing your fingers between the braces (or balance and brace) or by grasping the tubing on each side and pushing up on the brace with your thumbs. (To close the slide, reverse the procedure.) If unable to remove the slide in this manner, try the following method:

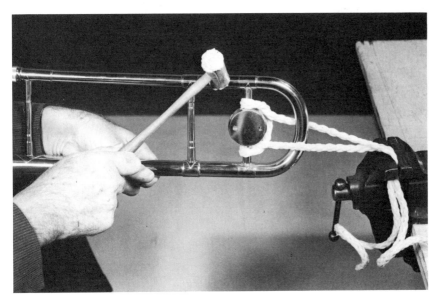

Photo 60

To correct: Using a new braided nylon rope (or soft substitute), place a double loop around the slide brace tubing. When the nylon rope is looped over the balance brace (*see photo 60*), each end is locked so it will not slip. Place the loose ends in a vise or tie them around a stationary object. Hold the bell under your arm; grasp the small end of the bell with one hand and tap the tubing—where the slides enter—with your rawhide mallet as you pull. Be sure to pull straight out with equal tension on both strands of rope so that the slide will emerge straight. If just one side of the slide is stuck, shorten the strand of rope on the lodged side and pull straight out from anchored rope ends. This will give the lodged side additional tension and will not disturb the side that is loose. After the stuck side moves, adjust the rope strands to equal lengths so the slide will emerge evenly.

Outer Slide Lodged: If the slide section is lodged in the slide receiver (bell section) and the locknut cannot be unscrewed, place the locknut on firm wood and tap with a rawhide mallet. This will usually break the seal and loosen the screw. If the locknut can be unscrewed but the slide section is still lodged, *do not* try to remove it by twisting. You will only twist the braces loose and bend the tapered tubing (tube that extends from the slide receiver to the tuning slide). Try tapping the slide receiver with your mallet. If the proper tools for this procedure are not available, take the trombone to your repairman.

Sprung Slides: Sprung slides may be caused by students falling over their slides, setting the instrument down on the slide bow too forcefully, or carrying excessive materials in the case. If the slide action is retarded and you do not see any large dents, remove the slide from the bell section and sight down each side of the slide. If the slide is sprung you will see a bow or curve (*see photo 61*).

Photo 61

To correct: With your right hand, hold the slide end that fits into the bell section. Place the bow end on a bench or table and with your left hand apply *slight* pressure to the top of the bowed slide—along the entire length of the slide (*see photo 62*). If you use the

Photo 62

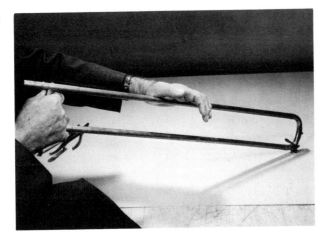

correct pressure and stroke, you will remove the bow or curve (*see photo 63*). If you use too much force, you will bend the slide in

Photo 63

the opposite direction. With a little practice you will be able to perform this straightening operation with ease and success. *Do not use excessive pressure*, especially if the slide is old, or you will collapse the slide.

TROMBONE QUICK-CHECK ROUTINE

1. See if the water key is bent off the water key nipple or if the water key cork is missing.
2. Check mouthpiece to see that the opening is not almost closed with accumulated dirt or corrosion and that the end which fits into the horn is round and not bent.
3. See that the slide bow is not unsoldered where it fits onto the slides.
4. Hold fingers over the open ends of the slide and move slide up and down to see if there is compression. If none, it has a leak.
5. See if the hand-slide bow or the tuning-slide bow is bent (dented) closed.
6. Look down through the inner slides to see if they are clogged with an accumulation of food particles, corrosion, or cold cream.
7. Run a flexible cleaning rod through the bell section to see that there is nothing in the bell.

CHAPTER

1⓿

FRENCH HORN

GENERAL CARE

The French horn—constructed of thin and soft brass, required to produce a quality tone—is a delicate instrument and should be treated as such. Therefore, a new French horn student should receive—at the very beginning of his study—complete instructions on proper care of his instrument. Since French horns appear so frequently in the repair shop—usually in poor condition caused by neglect—such indoctrination is all-important.

Following are essential guidelines in the care of the French horn:

■ Since this instrument has no water keys, pull and drain all slides after each use.

■ Lubricate slides frequently, for they are subject to greater use than the slides of any other instrument. Lubrication is also essential to prevent lodging; because of their delicate structure, French horn slides cannot take the strain of being pulled when lodged.

■ When the instrument is stored in its case, be certain that the case is placed in an upright position. The case should not rest on its side since in this position the horn slides are higher than the valves, which allows saliva to flow down on the valves, where it dries. The valves will then stick.

■ Caution students to be wary of the instrument's thin, soft metal, which can be dented very easily. Inform them, too, that removal of dents will stretch the metal, possibly affecting tone production and pitch.

■ Students should not attempt to remove lodged slides, valves, or mouthpiece, but inform instructor of the problem.

■ To prevent collapse of the rim of the bell, never lean on or put any kind of pressure on this part of the horn.

■ Never try to remove slides by placing the bell over your knee. In most cases, the bell will collapse almost instantly.

■ Single horns are built in F, with a slide for E♭. When changing to E♭, do not forget to pull each valve slide to the marking (ring) on the tubing for the desired position.

■ Exercise care when tightening the straps that hold the horn in its case. Straps should never be pulled tightly across the tuning slides since the slides may be bent or sprung in the process, causing the valves to bind.

■ The ends of the mouthpipe and mouthpiece are small and must be kept clean and open. Accumulation of dirt or foreign material will definitely impair the instrument's capabilities.

■ Mouthpiece should not be slapped with the cup of the hand when it is placed in the instrument, as this may lodge the part.

■ Check mouthpiece frequently to be certain it is not bent.

■ Mouthpiece should be secured when carried in the case; otherwise, tubing may be dented.

■ Books and other items should never be carried in the case; the instrument's soft brass will dent very easily.

PROBLEMS AND REPAIR PROCEDURES

Replacing Broken Valve String: All horn students should be taught how to string a valve, a process that was much simpler when good linen string was easily obtainable. Now, however, woven synthetic strings are used; thus, the tip enlarges when twisted to allow entry through the key's string holes. To prevent such enlargement and allow easy entry, hold the tip of the string in a flame; then quickly draw the burning part through a rag. As the string burns and melts, a pointed tip will form.

To install the valve string, follow these steps:

1. Cut a piece of string approximately 7 inches in length.

2. Tie a knot at the end, opposite the pointed end.

3. Direct the tip through hole *A* in the key from the opposite side of the valve stem:

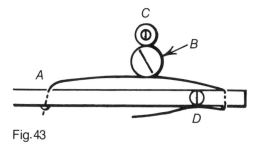

Fig. 43

4. Hold the spatula (pedal) even or level with the other pedals; extend the string to the valve stem (*B*)—on the side that the key passes—and then around *B* and onto and under screw *C*.

5. While holding the pedal even with the other pedals, apply tension to the string as you hold screw *C* against the cork stop.

6. Tighten the screw to secure the string.

7. Continue the string around the valve stem and through the hole at the end of the key; then loop the string around and under screw *D* on top of the key.

8. Tighten the screw to secure the string.

Removing and Replacing Rotary Valve: Removing or replacing a rotary valve is more complicated than the procedure for a piston valve. Care and know-how are essential to prevent damage. Therefore, study the illustrations of the assembled valve and its components before proceeding.

To remove valve: Release the string at the screws; then remove the valve cap (on bottom of valve). When removing the cap, note that the back bearing plate remains in the valve casing. Next, unscrew the retaining screw (screw in the end of the valve stem) about two turns and tap the top of the screw with a rawhide mallet; this will release the stop arm from the valve stem and also push out the bottom bearing plate. If the valve was causing trouble the bottom bearing plate will probably be lodged on the valve. Place a little penetrating oil on the bearing plate and turn it to remove.

Rotary valve trouble is seldom caused by the valve itself or by the valve casing, unless the casing is sprung. The culprits are the bearings: one is permanently installed in the top of the valve casing, the other in the plate at the bottom. These bearings fit tightly and prevent valve noise. When the instrument is placed in its case, the saliva runs back out of the slides and dries on the

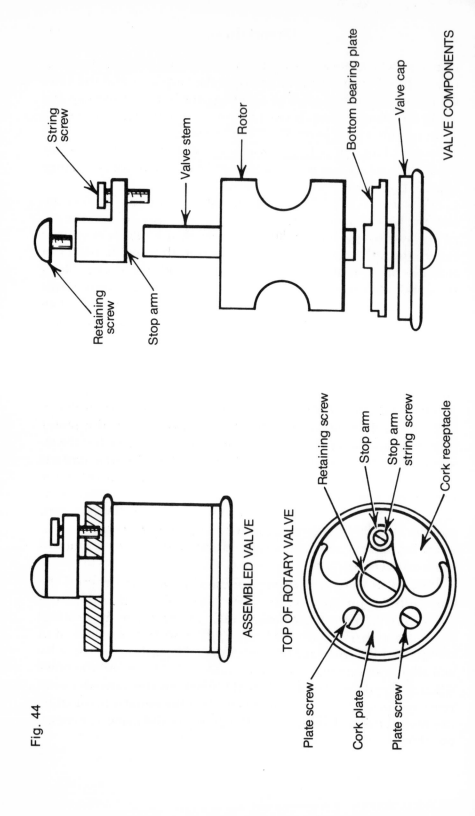

Fig. 44

String screw

Retaining screw

Stop arm

Valve stem

Rotor

Bottom bearing plate

Valve cap

VALVE COMPONENTS

ASSEMBLED VALVE

TOP OF ROTARY VALVE

Retaining screw

Stop arm

Stop arm string screw

Cork receptacle

Plate screw

Cork plate

Plate screw

bearings, which causes valve trouble. In most cases, the bearings can be freed by applying oil between the stop arm and the valve casing (for top bearing) or by removing the bottom valve cap and oiling the plate bearing. If you have to remove the valve, put some valve oil and a little jeweler's rouge on the bearing and then spin the valve. This will polish the bearing. After polishing, wipe the valve clean (*never buff or use an abrasive*) and apply fresh oil; then replace the valve.

To replace valve: First insert the valve in the casing; then install the back bearing plate. Note two small nicks—one at the top of the casing, the other on the bearing plate. Place these two markings together; then use the handle of a rawhide mallet or drumstick to gently tap the bearing plate into the casing, along the entire circumference of the plate. It must be installed evenly or the bearing will bind. Now, try to turn the valve stem. If it does not turn freely, the bearing plate is not straight. Check the plate to see if one side is not in securely. Tap again completely around the bearing plate as you continue to try the valve. When you get it straight or even all the way around, the valve will turn easily. After you get the rotor turning freely, replace the bottom valve cap. Next, replace the stop arm (note that the hole in the arm is flat on one side and round on the other; the valve stem is the same). There are also other types of valve stems and stop arms, but the inside of the stop arm will be of a design to fit the valve stem and will turn only one way. *Do not forget* to place the stop arm between the cork stops. Turn the valve with the flat side of the stem facing the area between the cork stops. Replace the stop arm in the same manner. Insert the retaining screw and tighten. *Do not* tighten this screw beyond the required tension, since most screws are made of brass and will twist off.

Inspecting Valve-Stop Corks: For maximum performance, the cork in the stops must be the correct size. To check if the corks are adequate, remove the bottom valve cap and note the bearing; there is one marking on the bearing plate and two on the end of the stem. If the corks are of correct size, the marking on the valve will align with one mark when the valve pedal is up and the other when the pedal is depressed. If the mark on the valve does not reach the mark on the bearing plate when the pedal is up or when depressed, the cork is too large. If it goes past the mark, the cork is too thin.

Freeing Lodged Rotary Valve: If a rotary valve becomes lodged, never try to break it loose by forcing down on the spatula (key pedal). Force will only break the string and, very possibly, break the key. Using a rawhide mallet, tap the retaining screw gently on top of the valve stem. This will break the seal (caused by saliva containing sugar that has dried and secured the valve) and the valve will move. To eliminate such sticking, saliva must be drained from the instrument each time it is played, either by pulling the slides and draining each individually or by rotating the horn until the saliva drains out.

Freeing Jammed Mouthpiece: If a mouthpiece puller is not available, lay the mouthpiece on firm wood and tap receiver with a rawhide mallet. Never use pliers, door jamb or pipe wrench to dislodge a mouthpiece.

Removing Lodged Slides: Follow procedure described in Chapter 8, "Cornet and Trumpet."

FRENCH HORN QUICK-CHECK ROUTINE

1. Check the mouthpiece. Hold it up to the light and look through it to see that the hole is fully open and that the end is not bent.
2. Check to see if the tuning slides are in their correct places.
3. See that the mouthpipe is clean inside and that there are no holes in it.
4. See that the valves are opening and closing completely.
5. See if any of the stop arm corks are missing.
6. See that the pedals are even and that the strings are tense enough so there is no lost motion in the valve operation.
7. See that there is no collected saliva in the tuning slides.
8. If a valve is sticking tap it on the retaining screw with the rawhide mallet to release the tension of the back bottom plate bearing.
9. See that the tuning slides are not bent or twisted.
10. Check the music lyre socket to see that it has not been bent in so that it practically closes the tubing at the point where it enters the 3rd valve knuckle.
11. See that there is no accumulation of foreign matter in the valve ports.

CHAPTER

11

SOUSAPHONE

GENERAL CARE

Mouthpipe: The sousaphone mouthpipe receives more abuse than any other part of the instrument and is the cause of 90 per cent of all repairs. Such repairs can be virtually eliminated by observing the following:

■ Keep the mouthpipe clean and polished, so movement of the part for adjustments can be done easily.

■ Remove the mouthpipe, bits, and mouthpiece when not playing the instrument. Remove them also when transporting the instrument. Have a padded bag with a drawstring made for these parts and tie the bag to the instrument so the parts will not be misplaced (a bag of this type is now available from various manufacturers).

■ Instruct students to loosen the ligature screw before moving the mouthpipe (rather than force it into position).

■ Keep the ligature screw lubricated with cork grease so it will tighten and unscrew easily.

■ Inform students that the brace beneath the mouthpipe provides slight protection for up-and-down movements, but the mouthpipe has no defense at all against forceful side action.

■ Make the student responsible for the mouthpipe. Further damage does not usually occur after a student is compelled to pay for a mouthpipe.

■ If several classes use the same sousaphones, issue mouthpipe, bits, and mouthpiece to each student for a fee. Refund the fee at the end of the school year if the parts are returned in good condition.

Other Parts and Procedures:

■ Do not overtighten bell screws; excessive force is not necessary to hold the bell firmly in place. If the bell screws are extremely tight, the instrument can be damaged in two ways:

1. The bell-screw flange (part the screws enter) is soldered on the bell-receiving ring; and if the screw is tightened excessively, the tension will cause backfiring, pushing the flange loose. The force created by the screw is stronger than the solder.

2. The bell will bend so that it is no longer round and will not fit flushly in the receiving ring. This will eventually create a problem in keeping the bell secure.

■ Never lay a sousaphone down (bell down) with the weight of the instrument resting on the mouthpipe or valve stems.

■ When traveling, remove the bell and place the horn proper on the bell with a blanket between the two parts to prevent scratching or marring of the finish.

■ When using sousaphone stands, be sure that the instrument is placed on the stand in the correct manner. Caution students not to guess. Advise them to read the instructions that come with the stand or ask the salesman to demonstrate correct usage. Sousaphones frequently enter repair shops with the knuckles (part where the tube leaves the valve casing) battered beyond repair by the instrument stand.

■ If a sousaphone remains in a hot, dry band room all summer, but must be used instantly for a performance, wash out the entire horn with water. The instrument will respond much more readily.

■ Clean and grease the slides at least once a month. This will allow more efficient tuning and aid in the removal of saliva. Regular cleaning and lubrication will also permit your repairman to make repairs more quickly—and at less expense.

■ In handling tuba cases, the straps that hold the instrument in place should not be pulled too tightly—excessive force will spring the tuning slides and bind the valves. If a valve sticks, rest the tuba on its back, depress the valve, and *gently* lift up on the valve's tuning slide. In most cases, the valve will spring back.

PROBLEMS AND REPAIR PROCEDURES

3rd Valve Does Not Work: This valve is located in a vulnerable position and is subject to hard knocks. If it does not respond, remove the finger button and depress the valve to see if stem is bent to one side and binding on the valve cap. If this is occurring, raise the valve and straighten the stem by tapping it gently with a rawhide mallet.

Valve Cap Lodged: Tap the cap with a rawhide mallet (never use pliers or a pipe wrench) to break the seal. It will then unscrew easily.

Mouthpiece or Tuning Bits Lodged: Remove the mouthpipe and lay the lodged part on firm wood; then tap with a rawhide mallet where the lodged parts are joined. As you tap, rotate the lodged part to loosen it on all sides.

Blocked Tubing: If the sousaphone does not blow properly, check the second and third sections of the large tubing (the two sections next to the bell connection) to see if anything is lodged in them. There is no more tempting prank in a band than to throw something down the sousaphone bell.

Throwing objects into sousaphones has become such a problem in some schools that screen protectors are placed over the bells. These are made of synthetic screening (like that used today in some storm windows), with elastic around the edge to hold it on the bell.

To correct: Take off the bell and extend your arm down the large tubing. Sometimes you can reach the lodged object with your hand. If this proves impossible, hold the sousaphone with the large part of the tubing closest to the floor. Then, as you rotate the horn to the right, slap the tubing with your hand; if the object is paper or a sack of popcorn or something light it will become dislodged and fall out as you reach the part where the bell is attached.

Another method: fill the horn with water and, holding the horn so that the large tubing is on the bottom, move the horn back and forth to slosh the water. Then rotate to the right and drain out all contents to the bell ring.

If the water method fails use a piece of heavy wire (about the diameter of clothesline) and bend a small hook in the end. This wire should be long enough to reach the fourth section. Run the wire through the tubing to see if it contacts any object. You can usually grasp the object with the hook and pull it out.

Check to see if the mouthpiece is missing. It sometimes falls down in the horn and will move around to the smaller tubing. If it is the mouthpiece or some other solid object, take a drumstick and tap lightly as you rotate the horn. When you reach the place where the object is lodged, the pitch of the sound will rise. Hold the horn so some of the tubing extends down from the object and tap the tubing with a rawhide mallet to dislodge the object. Then rotate the horn to the right until it falls out.

Loose Mouthpipe: If the mouthpipe ligature refuses to tighten enough to make the mouthpipe firm, use a magneto file and file out part of the ligature (as described in Chapter 6, "Saxophone").

Loose Joint: If you have a fiber glass sousaphone and a joint comes apart, it has to be put back together with an adhesive which you can get from the manufacturer or the store from where you purchased the instrument.

SOUSAPHONE QUICK-CHECK ROUTINE

1. See if water key on main tuning slide is holding open or if cork is missing.
2. See if valves are in the right casings.
3. See if end of mouthpiece is bent to the point where it is almost closed; see if its tube is clean and open.
4. See if mouthpipe extension (the part the mouthpipe enters that extends to the first valve) has been bent to the point where the tubing is cracked and leaking.
5. See if the felts and corks are missing from the valve stems, causing the ports in the valves and the knuckles of the valve casings to meet incorrectly.
6. Check for valve trouble by lifting up on the tuning slide tubing that contacts the sticking valve to see if the tubing is bent and causing the valve to bind.
7. Check the port holes in the valves for objects or holes.
8. Check the holes in the bottom valve caps to see that they are not stopped up.
9. See if there is anything in the horn.

CHAPTER

GENERAL MAINTENANCE AND REPAIR PROCEDURES

CLEANING

Lacquered Instruments: The shine of a lacquered instrument is not produced by the lacquer. The instrument has been buffed to a high luster and sprayed with a protective coat of lacquer. When the lacquer wears through or comes off, the instrument tarnishes quickly as a result of oxidation and from hand perspiration.

The only way to restore the instrument to its original appearance is to have it refinished. Bare, tarnished spots cannot be shined and lacquered to match other parts of the instrument. The finish fades with age and the buffed spots will be lighter and brighter. To help preserve the finish, the instrument should be kept clean. Use a lacquer wax or a moist cloth to remove fingerprints; then dry immediately. Students should keep a soft cotton rag or a chamois in their cases to wipe off perspiration marks after each instrument use. A brass cleaning rag or brass polish on lacquer should *never* be used.

Silver-Plated and Gold-Plated Instruments: For silver-plated instruments or mouthpieces (*excluding flutes*), use baking soda as a cleaning agent. Place a small amount in a container and add water to make a "soupy" mixture. Using an old toothbrush, scrub the instrument with the mixture. Rinse with tap water and then dry.

This method will also clean *gold* plating. Baking soda can be used to clean silver flutes and saxophones *if the keys are first removed.* Never try to clean a flute or saxophone with a liquid while the keys are on the instrument—you will ruin the pads and rust the rods.

Silver, Silver-Plated, and Nickel-Plated Flutes: To clean silver or silver-plated flutes, use cotton flannel cloth and jeweler's rouge. Never use harsh cloth of any type, since silver is soft and scars easily.

A chamois is recommended for cleaning *nickel-plated* flutes. If a flute of this type becomes so tarnished that it turns gray, it will have to be buffed to restore its luster.

Plated Keys: Plated keys on clarinets and saxophones can usually be cleaned with a damp cloth or a dry, soft cloth. It is important to initiate the cleaning process while the instrument is new—and to repeat frequently. If you wait until spots appear, they are most likely perspiration acid spots, which are already embedded in the plating.

Old German silver keys that have turned gray will have to be buffed to restore their shine. The same is true of old rubber-type composition clarinets that have turned greenish brown.

Wood Clarinets: The body of wood clarinets can be cleaned by ragging with bore or olive oil. A little Tripoli buffing compound may have to be added to the oil. A bristle clarinet bore brush is recommended for cleaning the inside of the instrument. After using the bore brush, repeat the process with an oiled swab. A tapered cornet mouthpiece brush is recommended for cleaning the toneholes of the clarinet. Dirt and sugar (from sticky hands) can be removed with a damp cloth (water-soaked). Shellac on the keys or body of the clarinet can be removed by rubbing with a rag and denatured alcohol.

Piston Valves: The brown tarnish on piston valves, caused by stale valve oil, can be removed by using a good metal polish, such as *Porter's Friend.* Never buff valves—they wear fast enough.

Woodwind Mouthpieces: To clean composition clarinet and saxophone mouthpieces, use a mouthpiece brush with soap or detergent. Never "cook" or use hot water to clean mouthpieces—you will warp the facing.

Valve Felt: If the felt in the valve cap becomes dirty, take it out and turn it over. The same can be done with the finger button felt.

Pads: The best way to clean pads is to place a layer of rag between the pad and tonehole; hold the key closed; then draw the rag out. This cleans both the pad and the tonehole.

The biggest problem: Encouraging students to clean their instruments —and to keep them clean.

OILING AND LUBRICATION

Oiling and greasing procedures—as noted throughout this book—are extremely important. They not only help to insure peak instrument performance, but increase service life by eliminating rust, wear, broken springs, lodged rods, collapsed mouthpipes, lodged slides, jammed actions, broken braces, broken tenons— and many other conditions. Indeed, if all musical instruments were properly oiled and greased, the number of repair jobs handled yearly would diminish dramatically.

It is not enough merely to tell students to oil and grease their instruments—they must be reminded and encouraged.

Consult each instrument section for proper oiling and lubrication methods.

SOLDERING

Procedure: *Never* use a resin-core solder or soldering iron to solder a musical instrument—you will merely pile on solder. Instruments must be sweat-soldered (capillary action); the seal produced by this method provides the strength to hold properly. The parts to be soldered *must be clean.*

If you want to solder a loose brace and cannot scrape clean the part to be soldered (because of its location), draw a strip of fine-grained emery cloth between the brace and the tubing as you hold the parts together. Reverse the emery cloth and clean the corresponding part. Remove the cloth and blow the dust off the parts. Next, take an old clarinet reed (it is thin and will pass between the parts to be soldered) and cover it with soldering acid (obtainable at hardware stores). Bind the parts to be soldered with soft iron wire (not too tight or you will dent the tubing). Heat the area to be soldered with a moderately hot flame; then draw the flame away from the parts as you touch the edge of the brace with wire solder (30-70) (some repair shops prefer 50-50). If the heat is at the right temperature and the parts clean and covered with acid, the solder will draw between the brace and tubing the instant you touch it. This produces a fine seal that will not come loose.

Difficulty in Securing Parts: If difficulty is encountered in soldering the brace, it is probably due to an excessively hot flame. If such flame is concentrated on the brace, it will cause the heat-expanded air to move away from the brace, taking the acid with it.

If the parts are not clean, the solder will not hold. It takes a little more time to solder when the torch flame is lower, but a better job will be obtained. There will be no excessive solder to scrape off, and no burned lacquer.

Clarinet or Saxophone Keys: *Never* solder clarinet or saxophone keys. The areas involved are usually so small that the solder will not hold. Solder is soft and will bend easily. Keys must be brazed or silver-soldered; this is a job for your repairman, since it requires equipment which is usually not practical for classroom repair.

Soft Soldering and Silver Soldering: The difference between soft soldering and hard or silver soldering is this: in soft soldering, two parts are united with a fusible metallic cement (lead); in silver soldering, both parts are heated red hot and borax is used as a flux, to fuse both parts with silver solder.

Soldering Facts and Tips:

■ If a saxophone post comes off and has not been separated from the instrument long enough for the solder to oxidize (turn black), merely apply acid between the parts and solder the post back on.

■ Lacquers now in use can stand a great deal of heat; therefore, if you keep your torch flame low and do not rush the work, you can replace saxophone posts, trumpet finger hooks, and other parts without burning the lacquer.

■ When soldering, the connection will be just as strong as the seal. For this reason, parts to be soldered must fit flush. If a brace flange or socket is bent, be sure to straighten it to conform to the part to which it will be attached.

■ *Never* try to spot-weld a brass instrument with an electric outfit. It will only burn the brass.

■ Soldering perfection requires patience and experience, but with a little practice it becomes rather easy.

CHAPTER

13

PERCUSSION

SNARE DRUM (Field Drum, Tenor Drum, Tom-Toms)

Drum head tension should be uniform. To accomplish this, measure the distance between the lug (part the tensioning screw enters) and the rim, and check that this distance is uniform for all tensioning screws. To keep the distance constant, mark a spot on the head at one of the screws and if you have to tighten the head, start at this marked tensioning screw and circle the entire drum, turning each screw the same distance (for example: half a turn). When you get back to the marked spot, you know that you have completed the circle and the tension is still uniform. Each time you tighten or release the tension, start at this marked spot. You will not only receive maximum performance from your drum, but the heads will last much longer.

By keeping the head tension uniform you will eliminate warped rims and shells and retain the best appearance of the drum. Tuned in this manner, the drum will also produce its most musical sound. When replacing a broken head with a new one, follow the same procedure.

If you do not use the drums during the summer and they remain in a hot, arid room, be sure to release some of the tension of each head.

All moving parts of both drum and stand should be lightly oiled at least once a year. If a field drum is used outdoors in the rain, all moving parts should be wiped dry and reoiled.

BASS DRUM STAND

Always use a stand or cradle for your bass drum. If the bass drum is set on the floor, it will rest on the hoop. Then each time the drum is struck, it will rock on the head, which is wrapped around the hoop. As a result, the head will soon wear through. The methods of tensioning the head and statements regarding oiling described for snare drum also apply to the bass drum.

CYMBALS

Never clean cymbals with a course abrasive. This will mar the tone quality and reduce the effectiveness of the instrument. If cymbal rouge is not available, try using a vinegar-soaked soft cloth, always using a rotating motion.

Leather handles should be used with band or symphony cymbals instead of handles affixed to the cymbals by means of a nut and bolt; the latter reduce resonance and form a rigidity that can cause cracking. Leather handles should be tied as illustrated below:

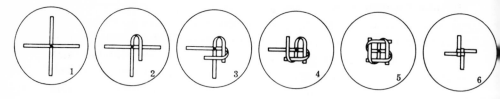

TIMPANI

The collar (distance the head is pulled over the rim) on the timpani should be about 3/4 inch for proper tuning. If the heads are made of calf skin and were recently used for an outdoor evening concert or in any other damp location, they have probably been stretched to where they are no longer tunable.

To correct: Remove the hoop with its mounted head and dampen the head thoroughly with a wet rag *(do not* wet the part which is tucked or wrapped around the hoop). Place the heads in an arid room and allow them to dry. You will find on reassembling the timpani head that it has shrunk to where it is again tunable.

The same procedure can be used on bass drum heads, but *do not* remove the heads from the shells or the wooden hoops will warp. Merely loosen the tensioning screws until the head is limp, then wet it down and allow to dry. Be sure the tensioning screws are loosened the same distance so the hoop and rim will not warp. Do not wet the part of the head which is tucked around the hoop. This procedure is *not* needed for plastic heads.

If a squeaking sound is heard when tightening the tension of a timpani head, it is usually caused by the head rubbing across the edge of the bowl of the drum. Remove the head and put a light coating of paraffin on the edge of the bowl and then replace the head. The method of tensioning the head and statements regarding oiling described for snare and bass drum also apply to the timpani.

For pedal timpani to function properly, they must be accurately tuned to their fundamental pitch with the pedal in the low note position. Failure to do this will make it impossible to utilize the entire range of the instrument.

KEYBOARD (Bar) PERCUSSION (Glockenspiel, Bell Lyra, Xylophone, Vibes, Marimba, Chimes)

If the bars or tubes on your instrument lose their quality, it is usually due to a bent screw or pin binding the bar and preventing it from vibrating freely. The glockenspiel and bell lyra have a rubber bushing between the bar and the screw. The screw goes through a threaded hole in the frame and is then anchored firmly on the back by two nuts and a lock washer. Occasionally, the screw is tightened too much and binds the bar. To remove the screw, dismantle the two nuts and lock washer with pliers, then remove the screw with a screwdriver. If the screw is bent, the bar will move from side to side or up and down and bind. A bent screw must be replaced. To produce the desired resonance, the bar must be free.

Xylophone, vibe, marimba and chime bars and tubes are mounted on a string which either rests upon or goes through a supporting pin. These pins may be bent, thus causing bar vibration to be hampered. These pins may be straightened with pliers. The motor of a vibe and all moving parts of both the vibe and chimes should be oiled periodically.

APPENDIX

REPAIRING INSTRUMENT CASES

In the past, instrument cases presented few problems; most of them outlasted the instrument. They were made of wood or plywood and could be repaired. If you have such cases, take good care of them; if they are damaged, repair them promptly.

Today, case manufacturers change styles and models frequently, making it impossible to comment here on particular types. Nevertheless, the examples described here will point out—and provide remedies for—a number of common problems.

Photo 64

REPAIR PROCEDURES

Damaged Case: It might seem that the trombone case shown in photo 64 is beyond repair, but in fact it can be restored easily and inexpensively.

Procedure:

Photo 65

1. Use an old saxophone reed to apply wood glue between the layers of loose veneer, and between the veneer and end section, which is usually solid wood (*see photo 65*). If the end section is loose, anchor it to the veneer with small brads. If the veneer is in such poor condition that it does not conform to the case shape, wrap a piece of stovepipe wire completely around the case and twist until it pulls the veneer down in place. Allow to set until dry.

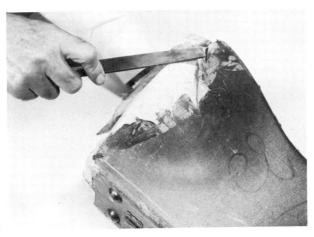

Photo 66

2. Fill the cavity with plastic wood and shape as it appeared originally; then let dry. File the surface smooth (*see photo 66*). If a higher quality job is desired, use fine-grade sandpaper and sand until smooth. (The case illustrated did not require a great deal of time to repair.)

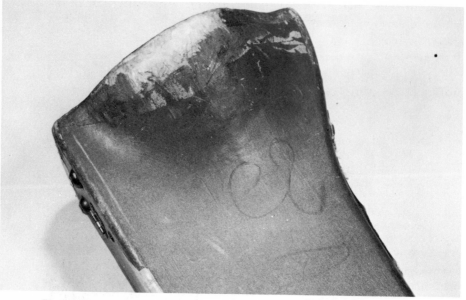

Photo 67

3. Use liquid shellac to attach the frayed or loose case covering. Smooth out the wrinkles and affix the edges of the case covering with your fingers (*see photo 67*).

Photo 68

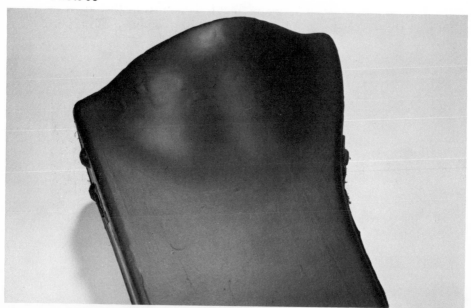

4. Spray with Nicholas #15 rubber lacquer (*see photo 68*).

Additional years of service can now be obtained at only about 5 per cent of the cost of a new case.

Loose Binding: The stitching on leather-bound cases often wears and breaks, allowing the binding to come loose. This usually starts at the corners. Such damage can be repaired very easily and should be done as soon as the binding comes loose—before it stretches, tears, or frays.

Procedure:

1. Apply shellac with an old reed; it is thin and will go back under the binding (*see photo 69*).

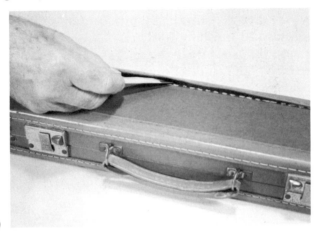

Photo 69

2. After covering the materials with shellac, force them together; either hold them with your fingers until they set, or place a flat piece of wood on them and hold down with a weight. Shellac must be used because it is waterproof. Never use glue or any adhesive that is water-soluble—it will loosen when exposed to

Photo 70

moisture or rain. Shellac also dries and sets fast, taking only a few minutes for the case to look like new (*see photo 70*).

Loose Covers, Linings, and Other Parts: If the case covering comes loose, it can be secured with shellac in the same way the binding was repaired.

The inside lining can be reglued since it is protected from moisture. Shellac can be used, but it is more expensive. Place glue on the case proper as well as on the lining—then hold in place with thumbtacks. After it dries, remove the tacks.

The accessory box in a saxophone case usually loosens when students set the case down with too much force. To reattach accessory boxes, holding blocks, etc., the parts should be glued where they were originally, but secured with screws. Use oval-head screws and finishing washers.

Sliding Catches: Sliding catches on flute cases cause considerable trouble, but can be easily remedied merely by applying a little oil to the lip or tongue of the moving part (*see photo 71*).

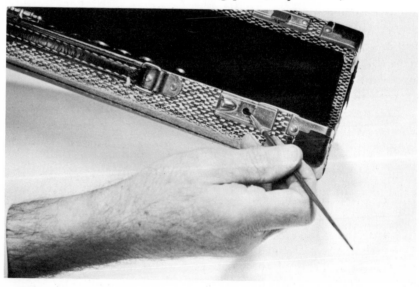

Photo 71

Case Locks: When the loop part of a case lock will not catch or stay closed, *gently* (too much force will break it off) bend the extension or lip down with flatnose pliers (*see photo 72*). This usually requires only very little movement, so bend in degrees.

Photo 72

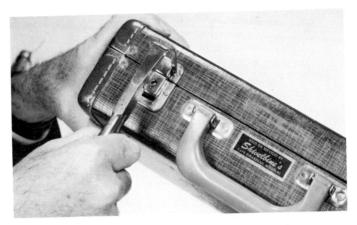

Broken Hasp: The part of the case hardware that provides the most trouble is the spring in the hasp (top part). When broken, the spring itself cannot be repaired; the entire hasp must thus be replaced. Since it is attached with split rivets, it is not too difficult to replace.

Procedure: With a screwdriver, raise the bent rivet ends that are inside the case. Then, press the ends together with pliers so they will retract easily. Force a screwdriver between the case and hasp base and pry loose from the case. To install a new hasp, place the rivets through the hasp base and case holes, from which the old ones were just removed. Next, spread the ends and flatten them out with pliers.

Case Handles: A replacement is obtainable for any broken, worn, or lost case handle. Most repair shops carry them in stock and can install them in just a few minutes. Or you can replace the handles yourself.

Procedure: To remove the old handle (ring type), use two pairs of pliers to spread the rings until they come out of the ring base. Spread the rings on the new handle in the same way, so that they are open enough to enter the ring base (handle comes with rings); then press them together.

If the handle is of the post type, remove the pin (part that extends between the upright posts, on which the handle is looped). One end of the pin is knurled so that it will bind in the post and remain in place. To remove the pin, grip it with side-cutting pliers. Span another pair of pliers from the post to the gripping pliers and apply force. This will remove the knurled side of the pin from the other post. To replace the pins, span the opposite post to force the pin back in.

INDEX